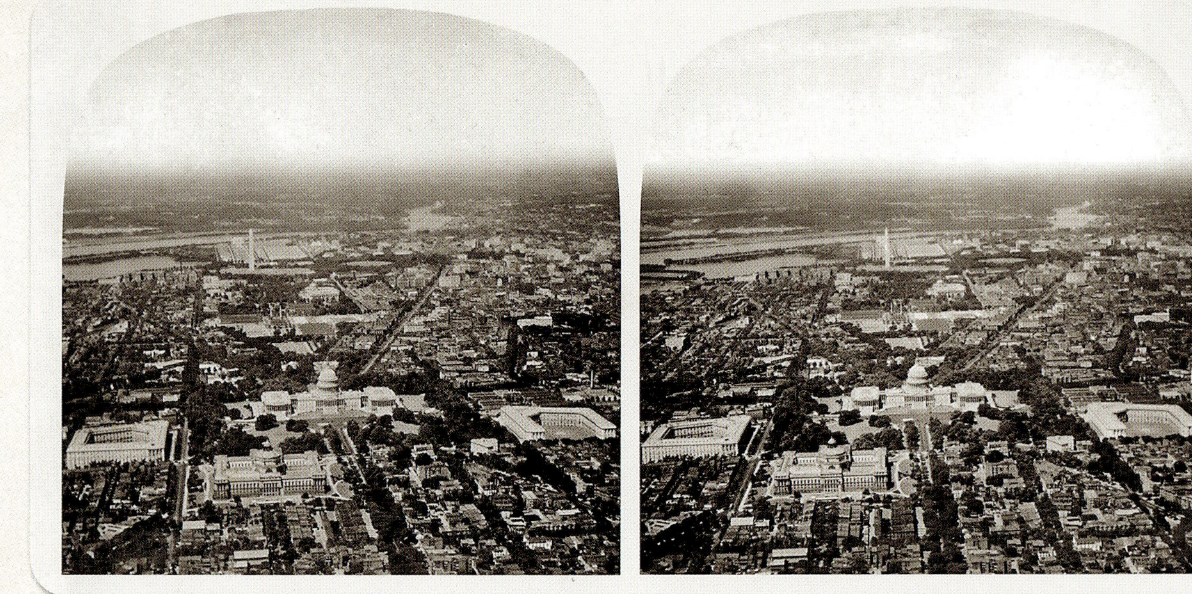

The monuments of Washington, D.C. are seen looking west over the city across the Potomac River.

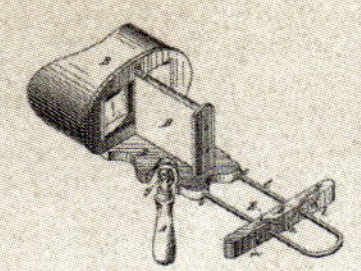

THE MARVELS OF STEREOSCOPY EXPLAINED

★★★

DESCRIBING DETAILS OF HOW STEREOVIEWS WORK AND INCIDENTS IN THEIR AMAZING HISTORY

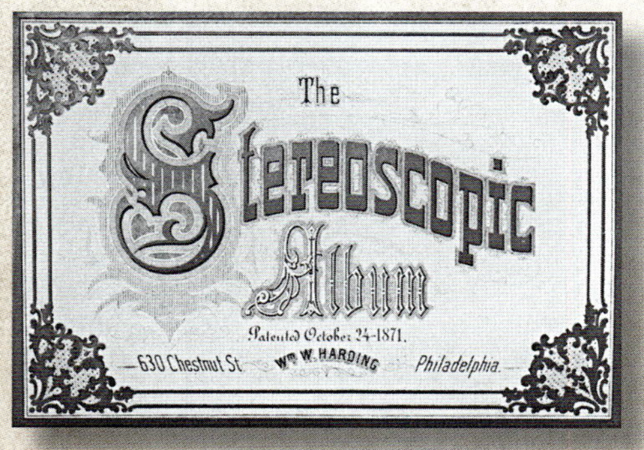

★ ★ ★

IN THE LONG-AGO DECADE OF THE 1850S, A MANIA FOR STEREOSCOPY flourished. Imagine, if you will, that the only images you had of the wide world were what you had seen yourself with your own two eyes. Newspapers and magazines printed only lithographs or engravings; photography was new and novel, a rich man's indulgence; moving picture films had yet to be invented. Then you were offered a stereoscope viewer and your choice of images, from the far-off pyramids of ancient Egypt to the fabled Great Wall of China. Peering through the viewer's lenses, suddenly the wonders of the world were there before you in all their three-dimensional glory. It was as if those sites and the people depicted were alive and breathing there in front of your own two eyes!

Stereoviews were the television or internet of the day. At the peak of their popularity from the 1850s through 1930s, a stereoscope viewer and a carefully chosen collection of stereoviews boasted pride of place in most every middle- and upper-income household around the globe. Stereoviews offered entertainment, education, and armchair travel all in one. They were the virtual reality of their day and age.

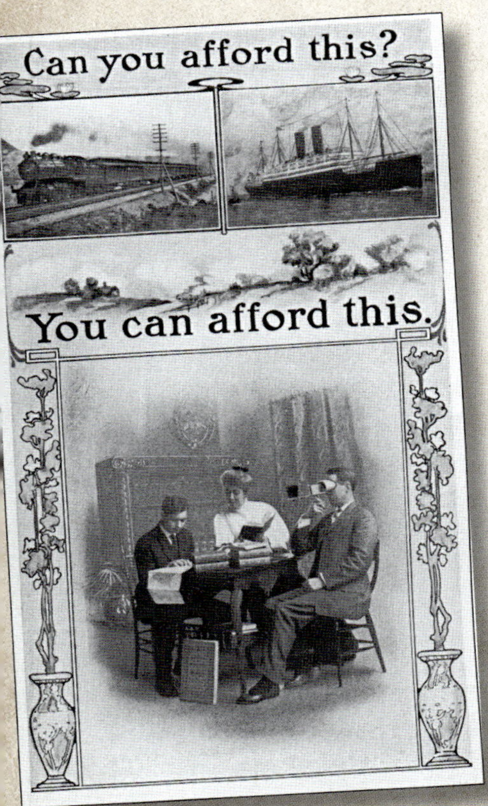

The invention of stereoscopy coincided with our comprehension of the concepts of binocular vision and the separate development of photography. In 1838, British scientist Sir Charles Wheatstone presented a paper to the Royal Society demonstrating stereopsis and explaining that we perceive objects in three dimensions because each eye sees a slightly different view; our brains reconcile the two images into one three-dimensional image. Wheatstone unveiled a crude stereoscopic viewer using angled mirrors to look at

★ ★ ★

drawings. But it wasn't until the 1851 International Exhibition at London's Crystal Palace that everyday people could try out Scottish scientist Sir David Brewster's "improved" binocular stereoscope. Queen Victoria herself proclaimed the stereoscope a marvel of the highest order.

And thus the fad began. From the early 1850s to the late 1930s, millions of stereoscopic images were made by both commercial and amateur photographers. Famous publishers such as Underwood & Underwood, Keystone View Company, B. W. Kilburn, and many more soon began issuing stereoview collections. They documented famous personalities of the times, landmarks around the globe, bible stories brought to life, scientific principles from zoology to astronomy, cycloramas of historical occurrences, and the era's current news events, from the American Civil War and San Francisco's 1868 and 1906 earthquakes to the horrors of World War I. There were even risqué boudoir views available, if you knew who to ask.

Images were on sale at tourist attractions as souvenirs to wow the folk back home. Traveling salesmen carried their cases of wares from door to door, offering viewers and photos to discerning fans eagerly building their collections. Stereoviews provided many people their first photographic views of the world, and they became devoted fans.

By the 1930s, stereoscopy was suddenly old-fashioned and out of fashion. Newspapers now reproduced photographic images, and the new marvels of moving pictures and newsreels brought the world to people in the comfort of theater palaces. The wonders of those once-amazing stereoviews had been surpassed.

But here, in this album of near-forgotten stereoviews, the past lives and breathes once again—in 3D!

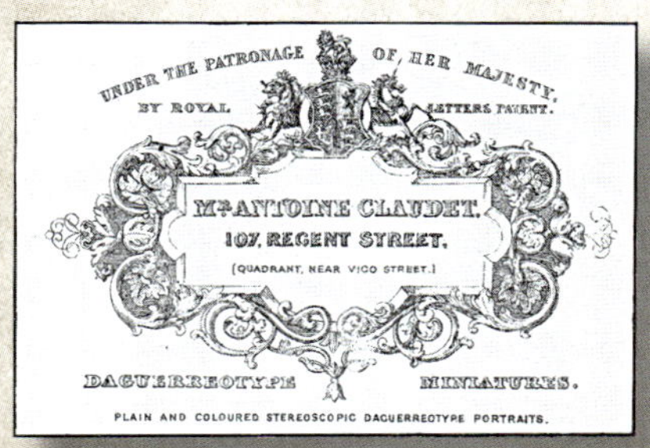

⋆⋆⋆

HOW TO USE THE STEREOSCOPE VIEWER

Relax, and Travel Back in Time!

IN THE EARLY DAYS OF STEREOSCOPY, PHOTOGRAPHERS CREATED the novelty of stereoviews by taking an initial photograph, then moving their camera slightly to a new position to snap the second image. Some inventive photographers soon crafted their own rigs with two, side-by-side cameras. Others used newfangled cameras with dual lenses spaced some 65 millimeters or 2½ inches apart—the distance separating the average person's pupils.

Looking through the lenses of a stereoscope viewer, the human brain recreates the three-dimensional view using the separate views seen with each eye. To do this, all you need do is relax!

To see the stereo image, do not force your eyes to look at the two separate images. Instead, begin by letting your eyes relax, looking above or below the images. Then, slowly move your eyes to the center of the images—and the two images will reappear in 3D. Once you have the images fused together into one, you can move your eyes around to examine different details of the picture and see it in all its depth.

If you wear glasses, try keeping them on while looking through the stereoviewer. The correction in your glasses is often necessary for you to focus on the images. But if it does not work, take off your glasses and try again.

If you're still having difficulties, try moving your head closer or further back from the lenses. You can also tilt your head left or right to adjust the horizontal alignment of the two images.

Simply relax in the comfort of your cozy parlor and prepare to be transported on a journey into the past with your collection of stereoviews and built-in viewer!

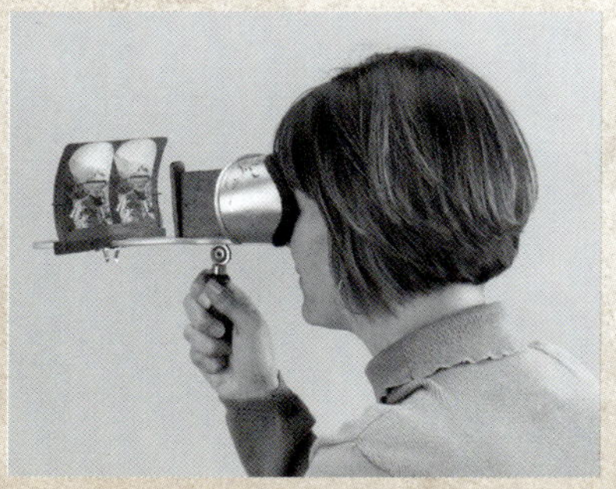

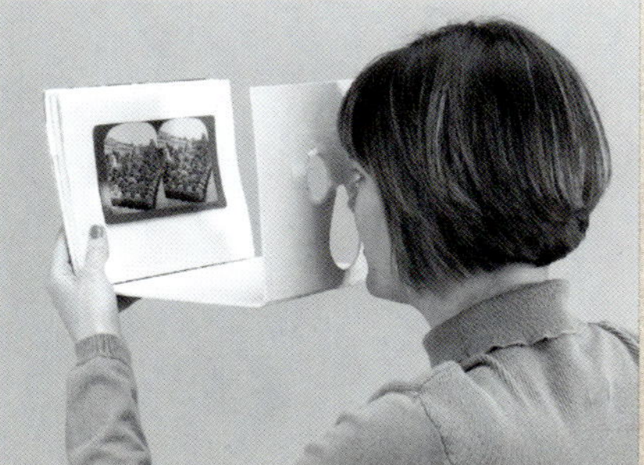

North from the Washington Monument

The south front of the White House is seen in the center, with 16th Street running north beyond it and Connecticut Avenue heading off diagonally toward the northwest. West (left) of the White House stands the official headquarters for the State, War and Navy Departments. The Treasury Department is located east of the White House, where the financial business of the country is carried out.

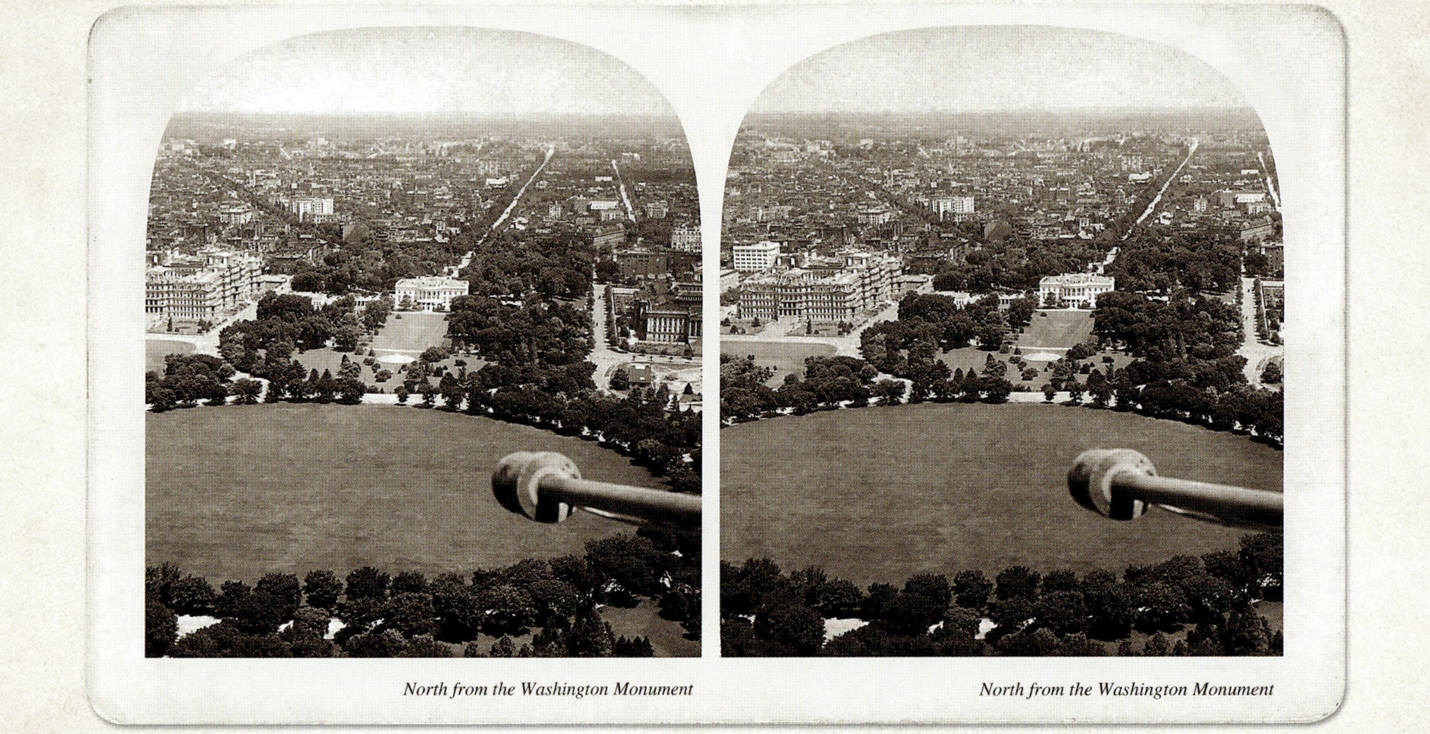
North from the Washington Monument

North from the Washington Monument

East from the Washington Monument

The Potomac River flows behind this vantage, and in the distance, the west front of the Capitol appears crowned with its magnificent dome. The brownstone buildings with their towers and gables include the offices of the Smithsonian Institution. Beyond the Capitol can be seen the Library of Congress. The large building just northwest from Union railroad station is the Central Market.

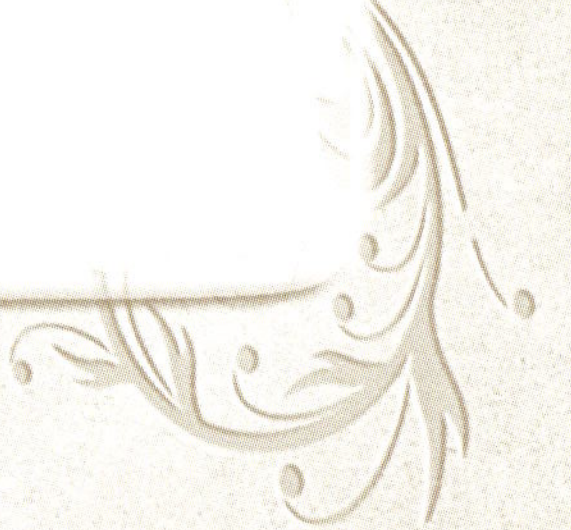

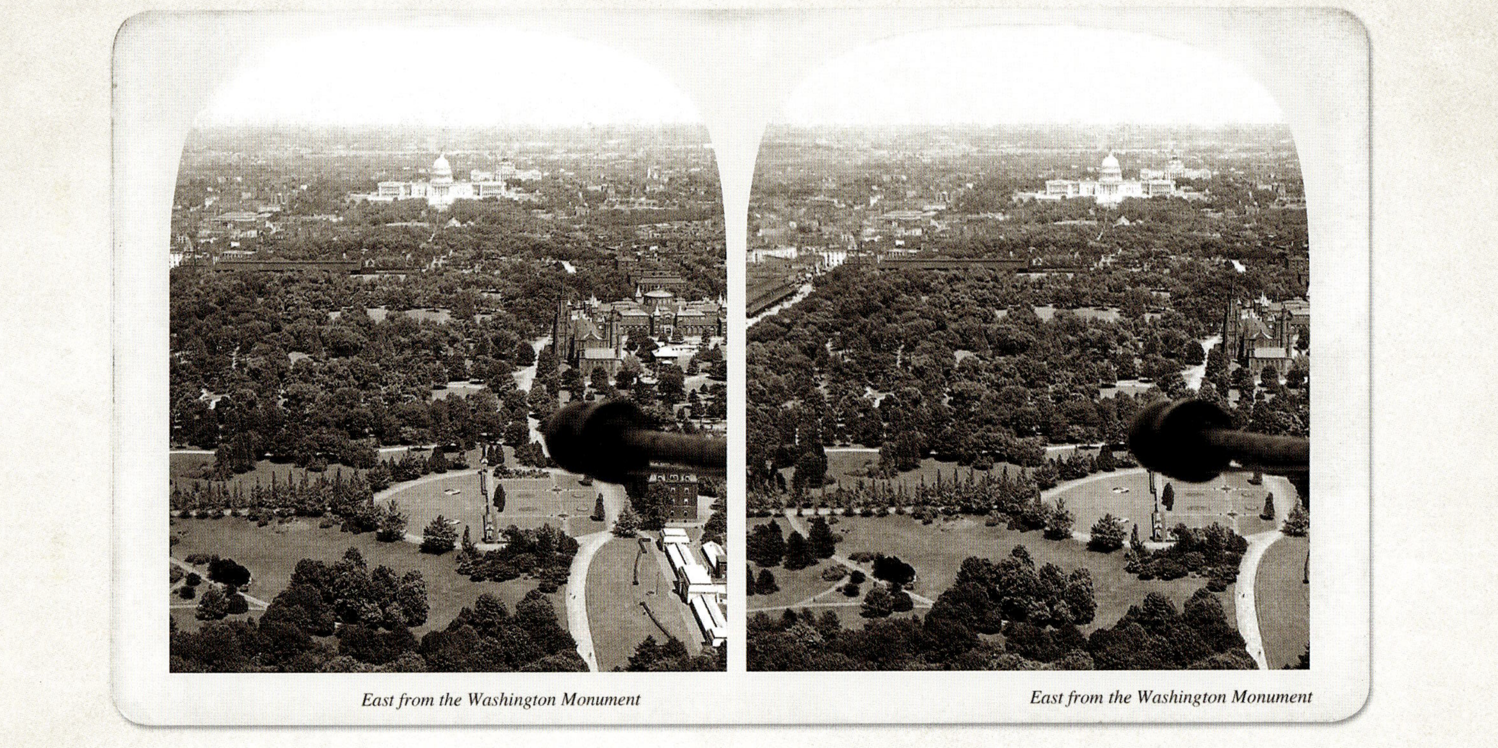
East from the Washington Monument
East from the Washington Monument

East toward the Washington Monument

In 1836, architect Robert Mills won the design competition for the monument to Washington. Mills' original design was later altered to the form seen here. The monument is built of innumerable blocks of stone, many donated by states and organizations to commemorate Washington. The obelisk has a height of 555 feet, while the base of the shaft is 55 feet square and the walls, which have to bear a tremendous weight, are 15 feet thick. Upon its completion in 1884 it was the world's tallest structure.

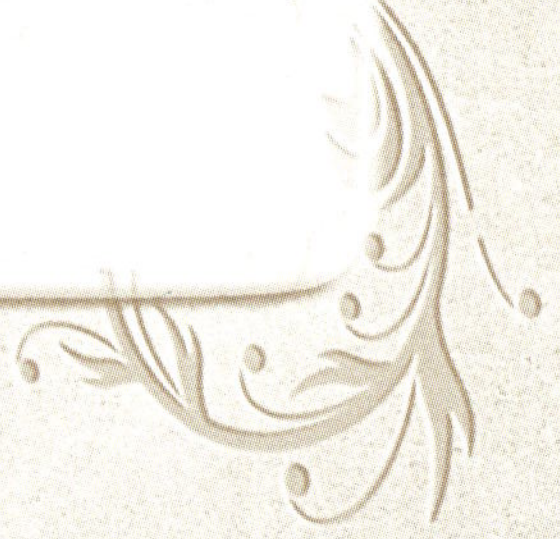

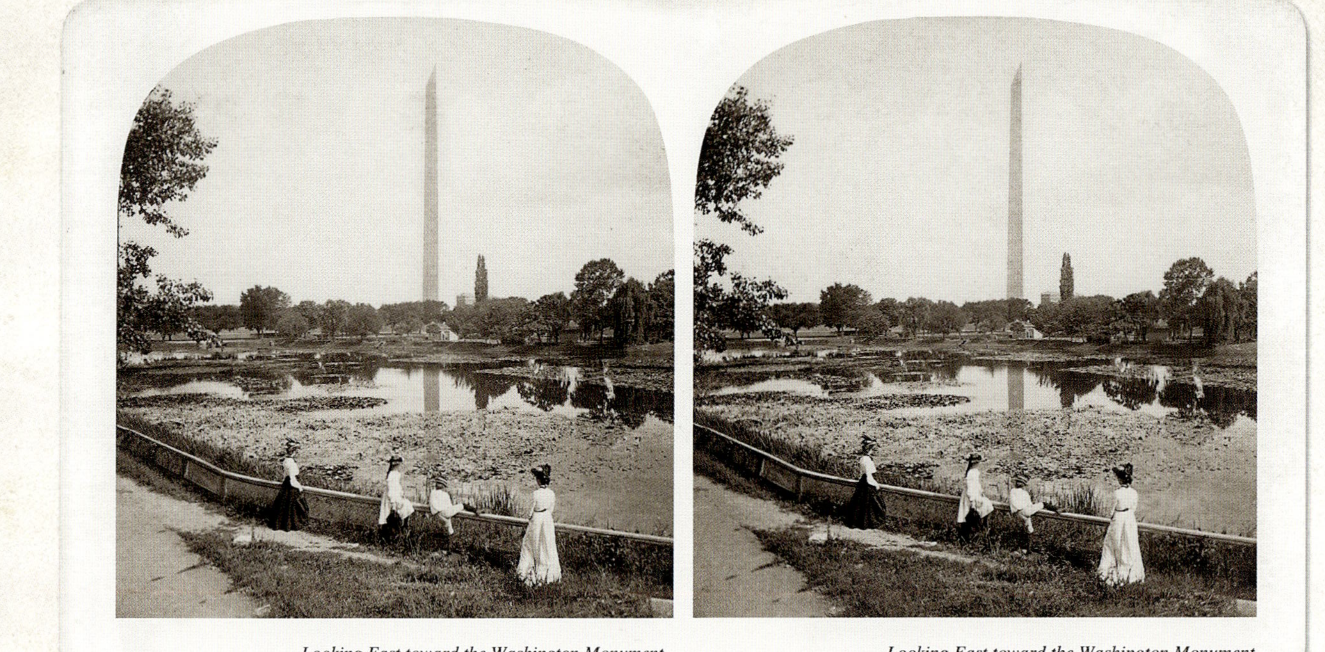

Looking East toward the Washington Monument

Looking East toward the Washington Monument

The Washington Monument

The cornerstone of the Washington Monument was laid in 1848, but it was not completed until December 6, 1884 with the setting in place of the marble capstone and its pyramidal apex of aluminum. The official celebration of the memorial's completion waited until Washington's birthday, February 21, 1885. At the dedication Senator John Sherman, Chairman of the Joint Congressional Committee stated of this tribute to our founding father: "The monument speaks for itself—simple in form, admirable in proportions, composed of enduring marble and granite, resting upon foundations broad and deep, it rises into the skies higher than any other work of human art."

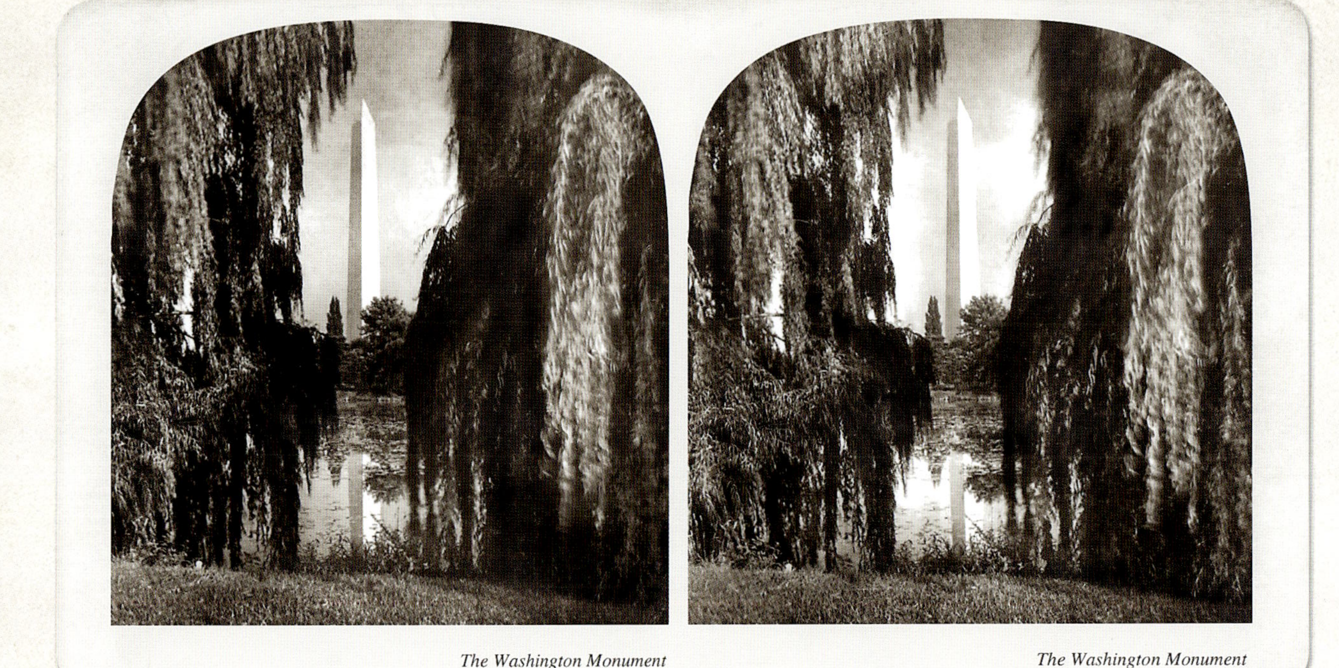
The Washington Monument

The Washington Monument

Mount Vernon, George Washington's Home

Mount Vernon, George Washington's home for over forty-five years in Fairfax County, Virginia, on the right bank of the Potomac, is situated on land that was part of an estate granted by England in 1674 to George Washington's great grandfather. Mount Vernon consisted of five farms known as the Mansion House, River Farm, Union Farm, Dogue Run Farm, and Muddy Hole Farm. While living at Mount Vernon as an ex-president, Washington carried on his interesting correspondence with Hamilton on the subject of federal union. In 1860, the mansion was taken over by the Ladies' Mount Vernon Association of the Union.

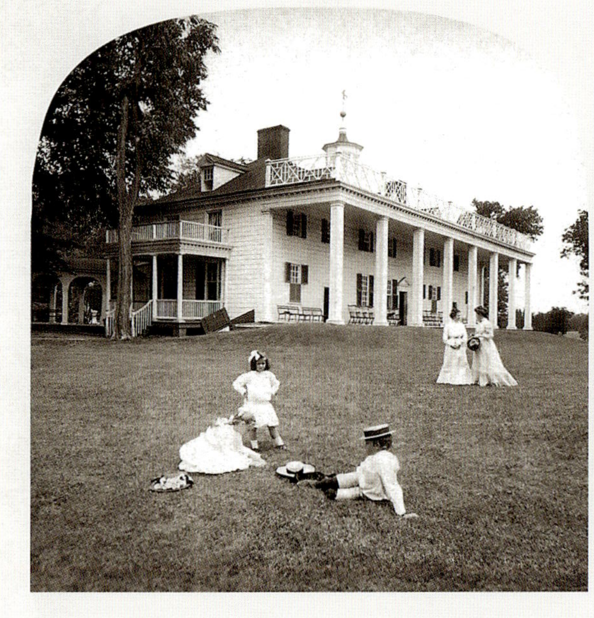

Mount Vernon, George Washington's Home

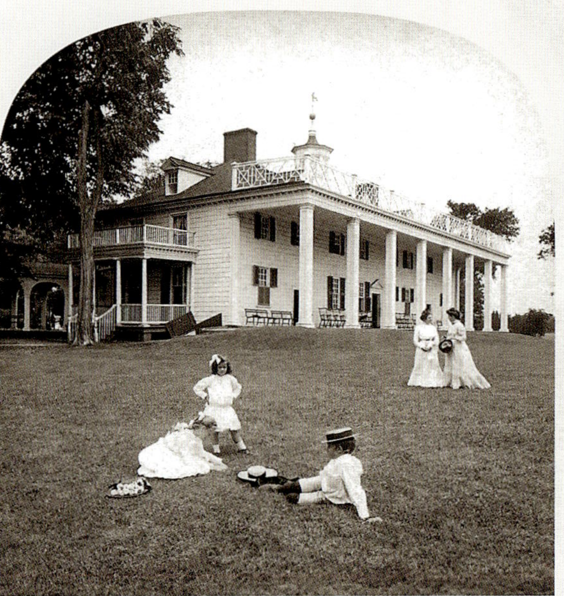

Mount Vernon, George Washington's Home

Washington's Tomb at Mount Vernon

Washington died in the master bedroom at Mount Vernon on December 14, 1799 and his will declared his wish to be buried there. Washington had also specified a site for a tomb to be built to replace an original burial vault. The tomb was constructed in 1831 and the bodies of Washington, his wife Martha, and other family members were placed in it. The inscription on Washington's tomb reads, "Within this enclosure rest the remains of Genl. George Washington."

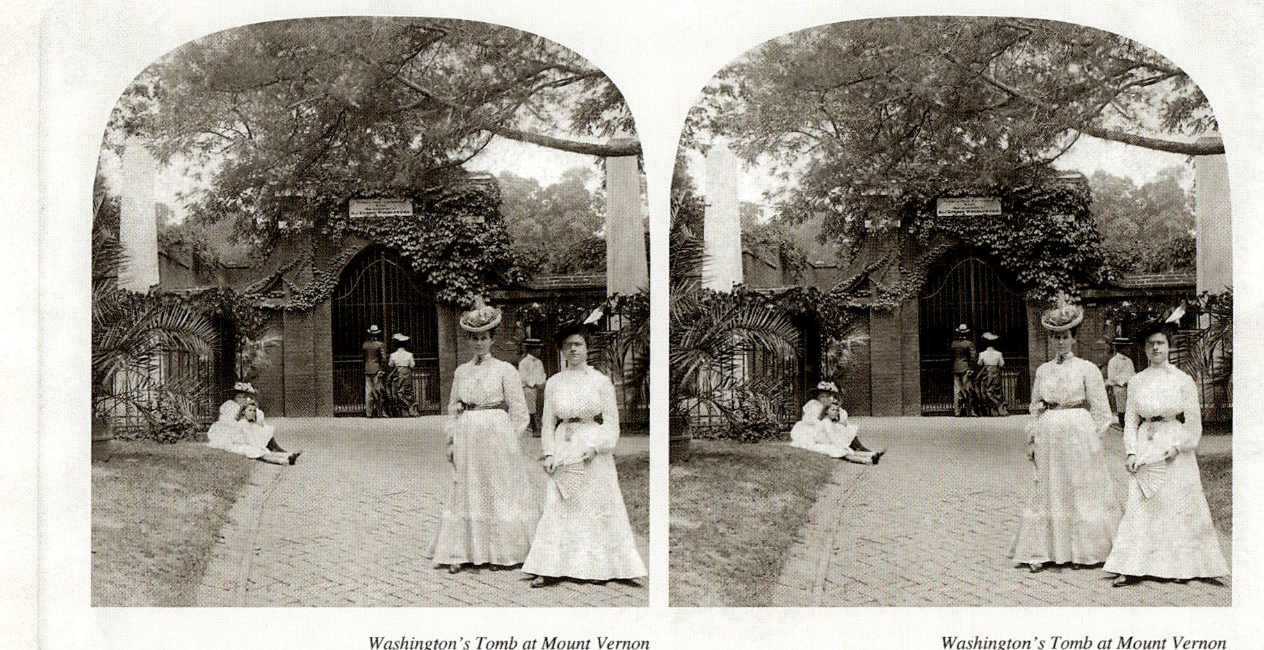

Washington's Tomb at Mount Vernon

Washington's Tomb at Mount Vernon

Abraham Lincoln

Lincoln was the first American president to be widely photographed, as well as the first to use the relatively new medium for political exposure. During Lincoln's first presidential campaign in 1860, a series of portraits by Mathew Brady were disseminated around the country. This portrait of Lincoln, taken at the Mathew Brady Studio in Washington, presents him seated in a pensive pose. It is a rare stereoscopic image of the president, one of only nine known to exist.

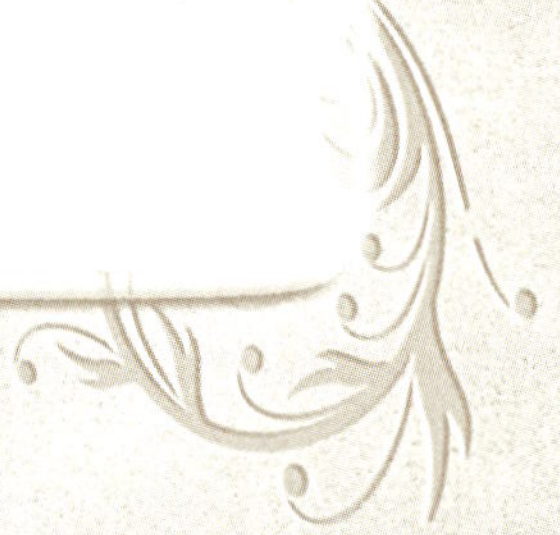

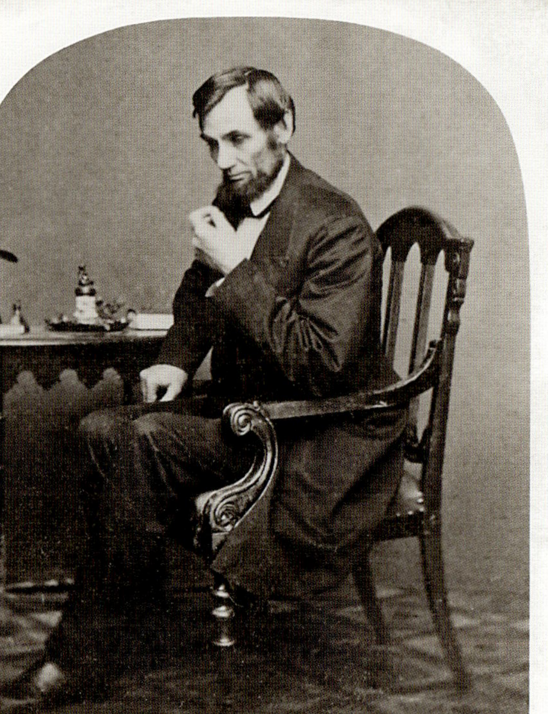

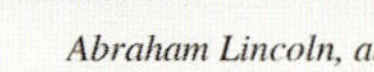

Abraham Lincoln, about 1862

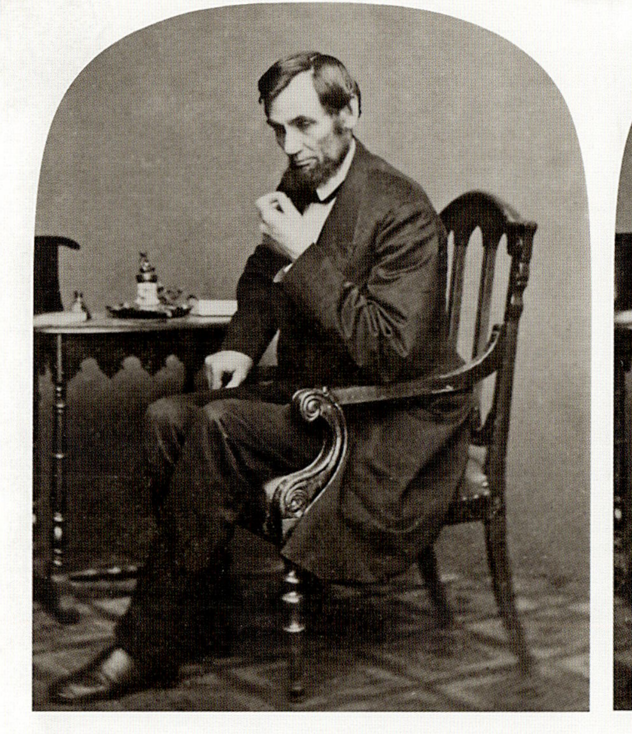

Abraham Lincoln, about 1862

Lincoln's Retreat

Located on the grounds of the Soldiers' Home, this cottage was used by Abraham Lincoln and his family as a retreat in the summer and fall. Located three miles from the White House, Lincoln often traveled between the two places on horseback, a forty-five-minute ride. Built in 1842, the thirty-four-room Gothic revival cottage provided a quiet refuge for the Lincolns during wartime. It was at this house that Lincoln worked on writings that would become the Emancipation Proclamation.

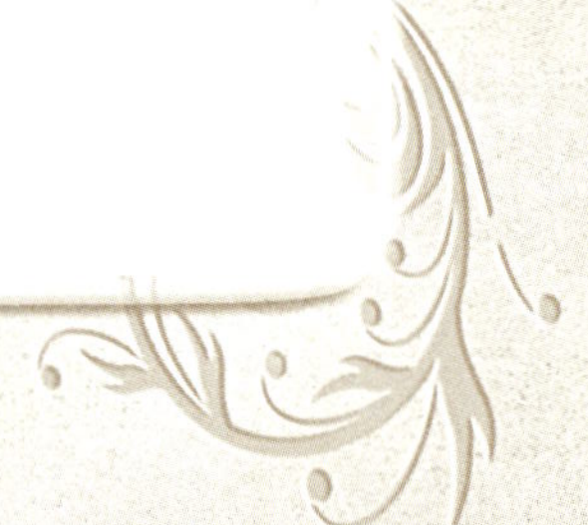

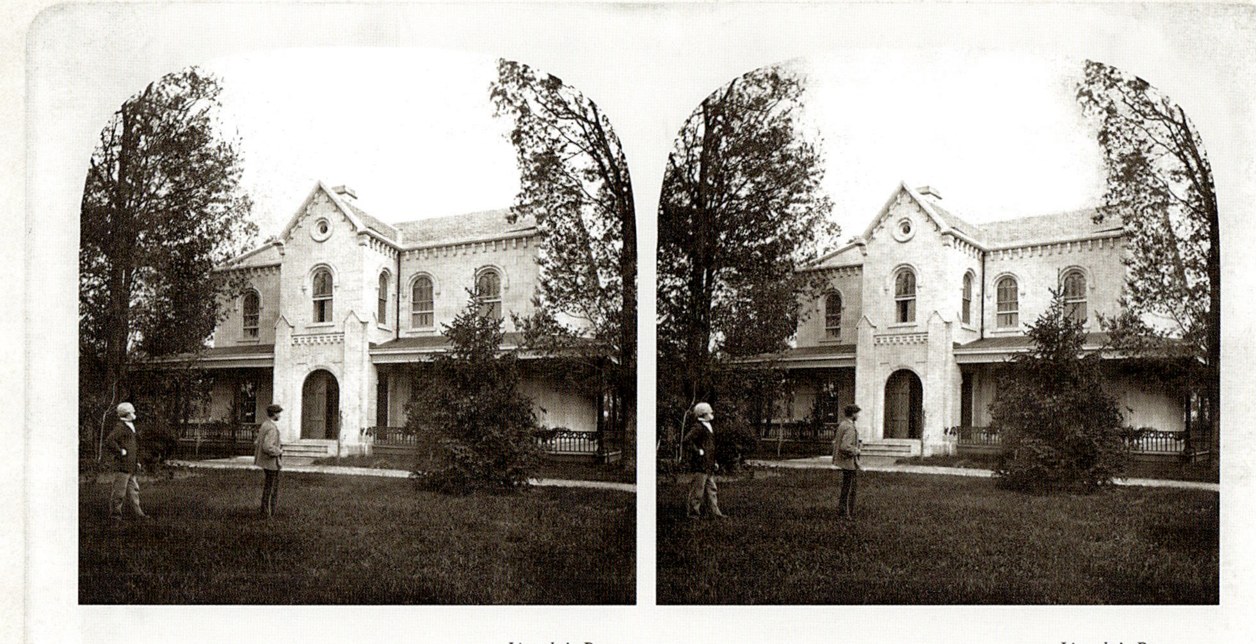

Lincoln's Retreat

Lincoln's Retreat

Examining a Pass, Mason's Island

During the Civil War, Mason's Island, readily available from Washington and Georgetown, served as a freedmen's camp for Virginia and Maryland slaves. Known at the time as "contrabands," the refugees required a pass to leave the island. Washington, D.C. guards examine a pass at this ferry landing on the Georgetown side of Mason's Island.

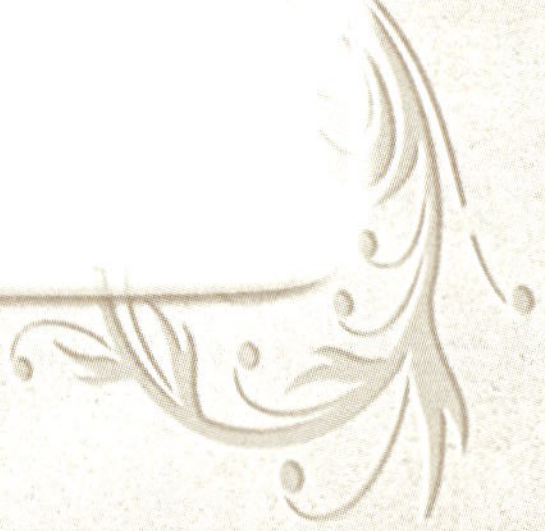

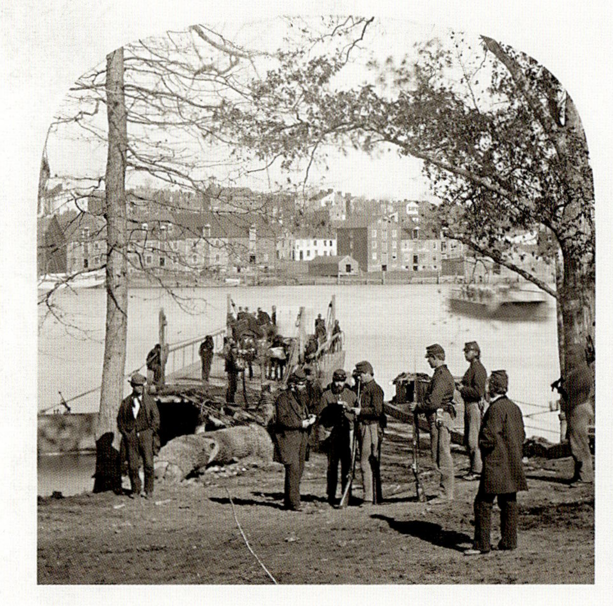

Examining a pass, Mason's Island

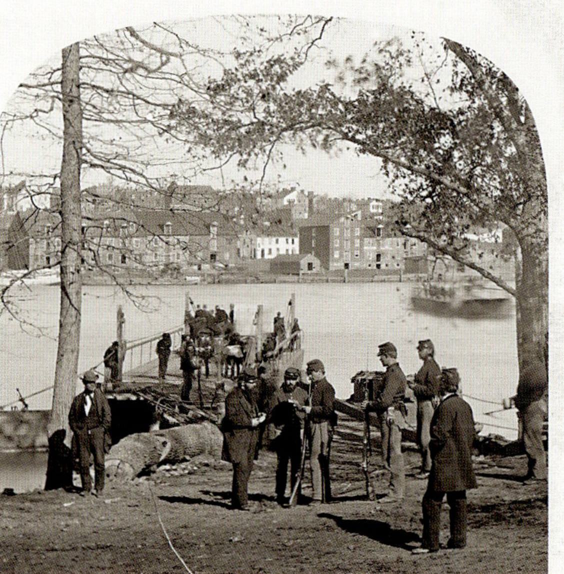

Examining a pass, Mason's Island

African-American Children

African-Americans are the majority of Washington, D.C.'s population. On April 16, 1862, President Lincoln signed the Emancipation Act that ended slavery in the District of Columbia, eight and a half months before the Emancipation Proclamation freed slaves in the rest of the country. These children are candidly posed in front of a building that is probably a schoolhouse. Shortly after the Civil War, Howard University was established in Washington, D.C. to provide higher education for African-Americans.

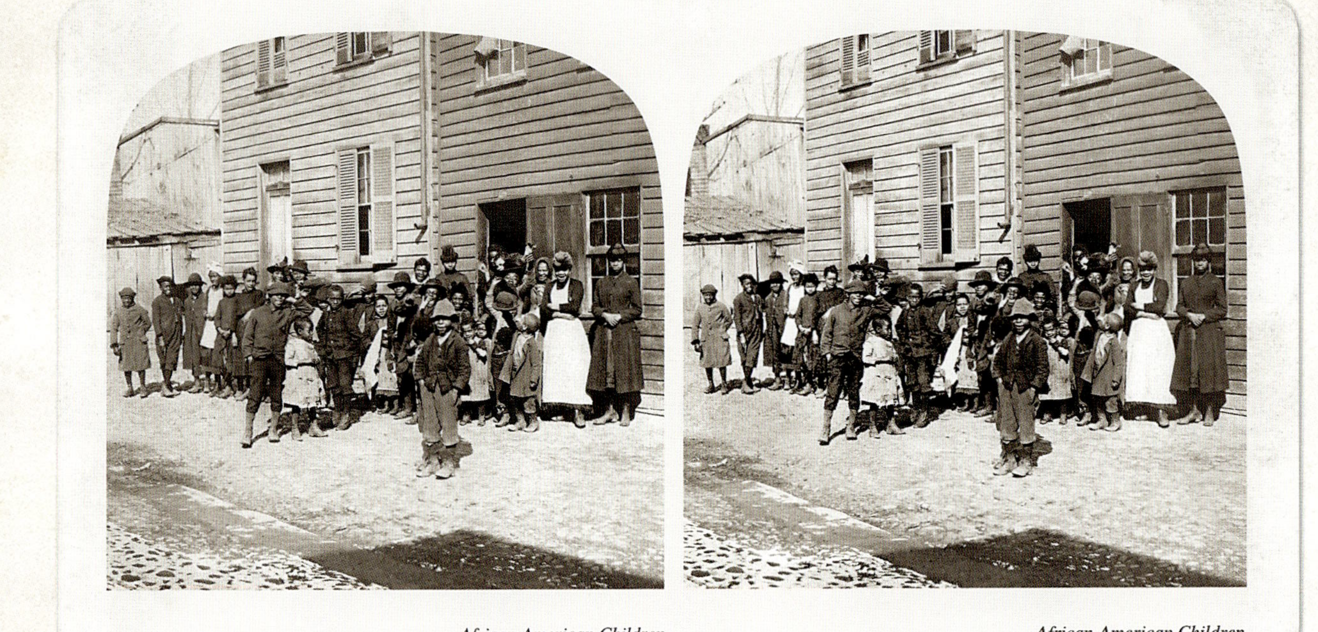

African-American Children

African-American Children

Ford's Theatre

On April 14, 1865, five days after the surrender of General Lee, Abraham Lincoln was sitting in a box at Ford's Theatre watching a performance of *Our American Cousin* when he was shot by John Wilkes Booth. Lincoln died the following morning at Petersen House, a boarding house across the street from the theater. It was the first assassination of a U.S. president. Booth was an actor who had performed several times at Ford's Theatre; after the shooting he fled but was caught and killed twelve days later. His fellow conspirators were tried and later executed. The first building on the site here was a Baptist church, but after the congregation moved to a new church the building was bought by John T. Ford in 1861 who changed it into Ford's Athenaeum and opened it as a theater. However, the following year it burnt down and when it reopened it was called Ford's New Theatre.

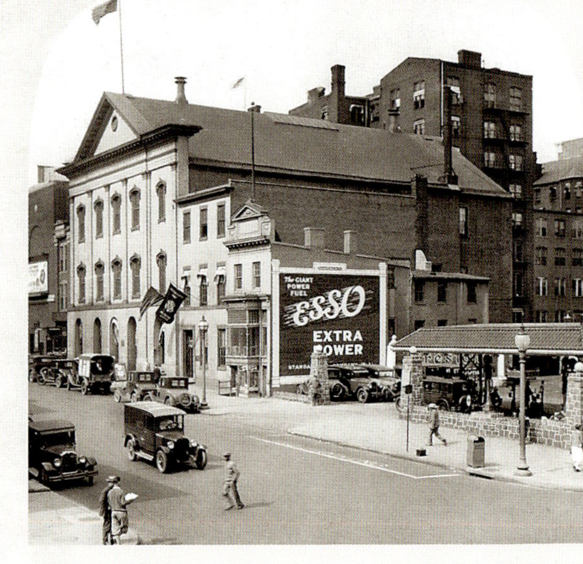

Ford's Theater

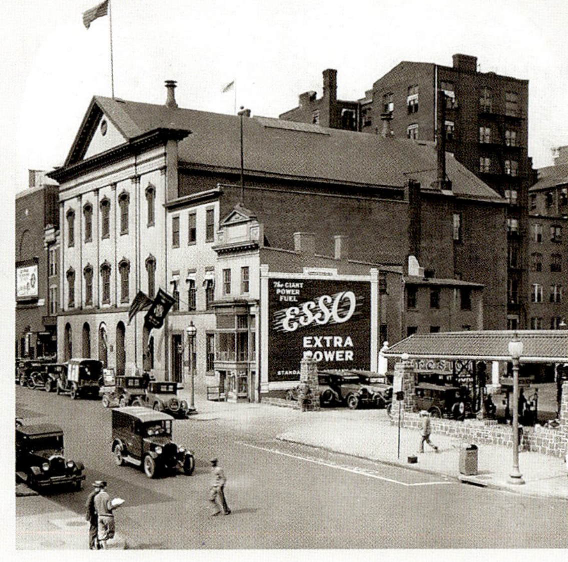

Ford's Theater

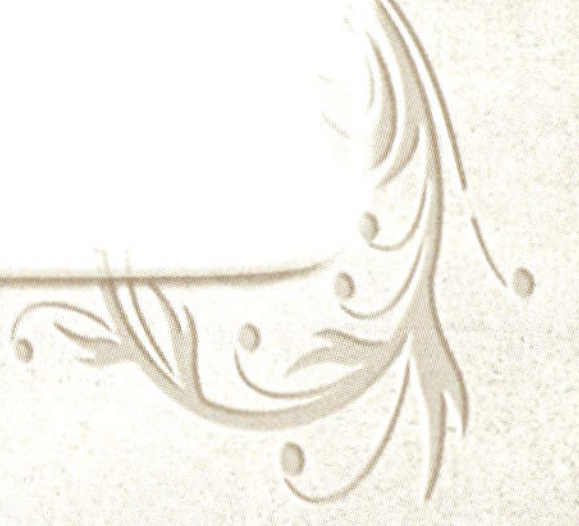

The Martyrs Lincoln and Garfield

Following the assassination of Abraham Lincoln on April 14, 1865, the nation's mourning took many forms. Lincoln, "the martyr of freedom," is presented in many photographic lamentations. This common style of mourning photography typically depicts the deceased, whether a family member or a prominent figure such as Lincoln or Queen Victoria, amidst a border of plants, flowers, and ferns. With the assassination of James Garfield on July 2, 1881, the country's two slain U.S. presidents were often grouped together as martyrs, with their depictions appearing in photographs, as well as in other mediums, such as a decorated mug. Later stereographs would include a third martyr, William McKinley, following his assassination on September 6, 1901.

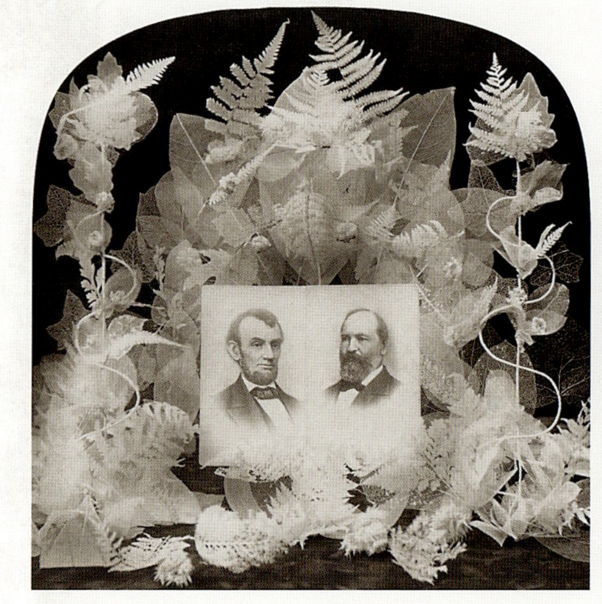

Stereoscopic Memorial to the Martyrs

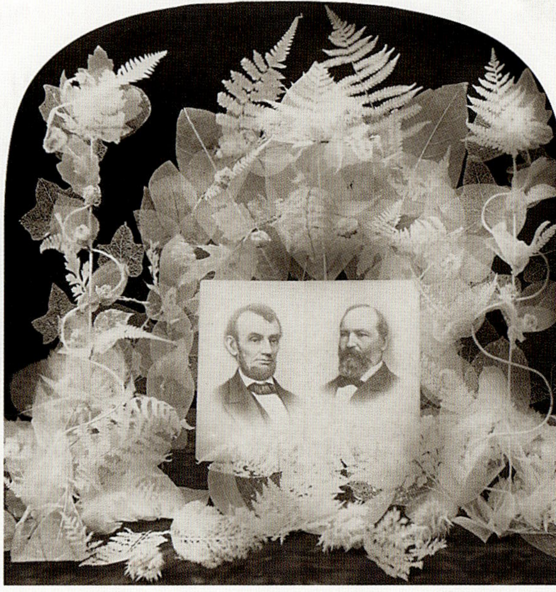

Stereoscopic Memorial to the Martyrs

Units of the 20th Army Corps, Army of Georgia

In May 1865, at the end of the Civil War, the victorious armies of the North marched to Washington, D.C. for a grand review. The Army of Georgia went by way of Richmond. On May 24th, passing on Pennsylvania Avenue near the Treasury, the men marched for their review before the president of the United States, Lieutenant-General Grant, and members of the president's cabinet, along with about one hundred thousand spectators lining the avenue. The soldiers of the Army of Georgia were united in purpose under the leadership of Maj. Gen. Henry W. Slocum.

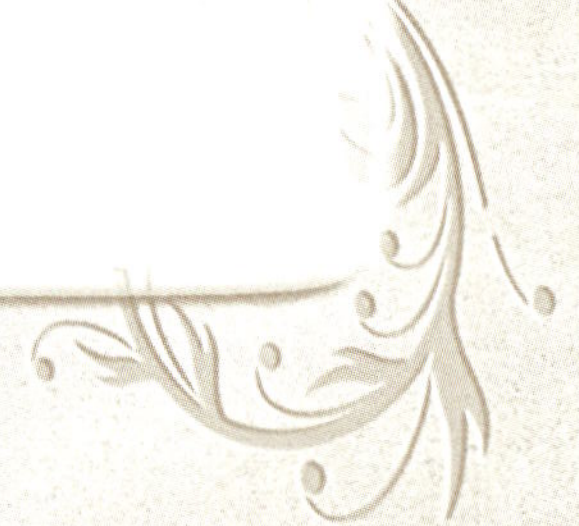

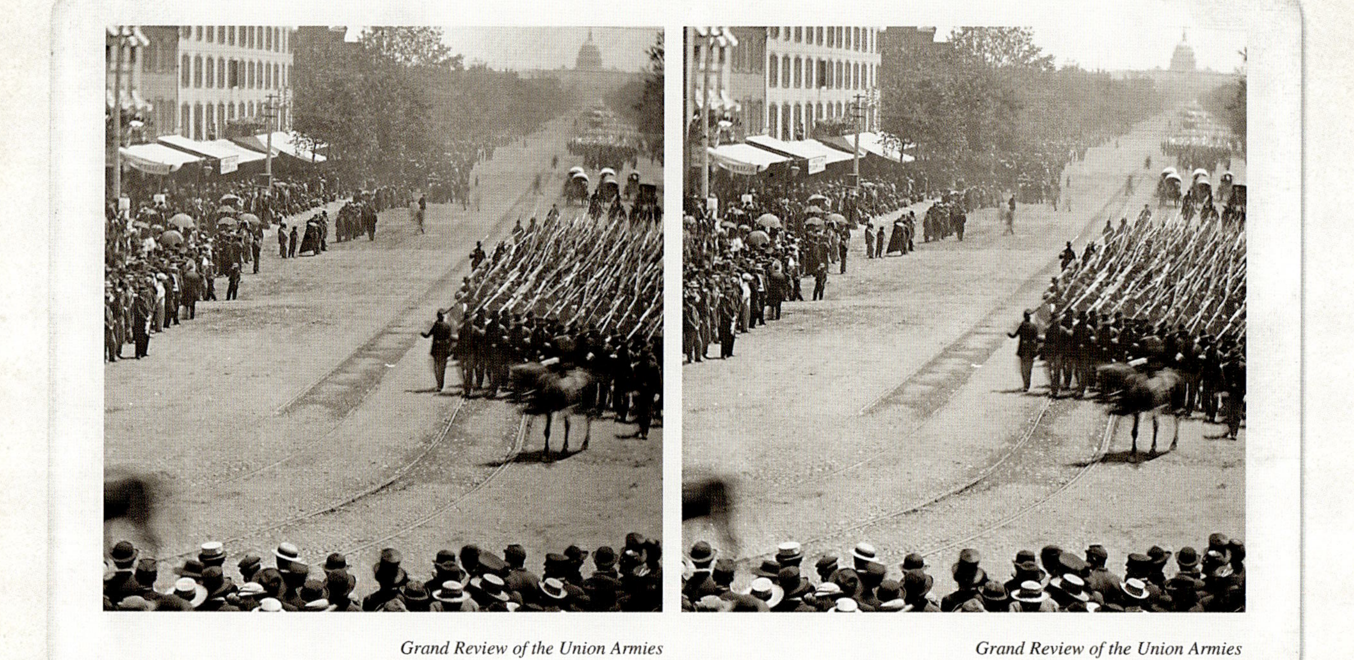

Grand Review of the Union Armies

Grand Review of the Union Armies

Lincoln Memorial

In 1922, fifty-seven years after the death of Abraham Lincoln, the United States erected a national memorial in his honor on the Potomac. The memorial, designed by Henry Bacon and built of white marble, exhibits simplicity and purity of line. Along its front is a colonnade of thirty-six Doric columns, one for each state in existence when Lincoln was president. Above, forty-eight festoons supported by eagles represent each state at the time the monument was built. At its dedication on May 30, 1922, President Harding gave an address, and Chief Justice William Howard Taft and Robert R. Moton, President of Tuskegee Institute, paid tribute to Lincoln.

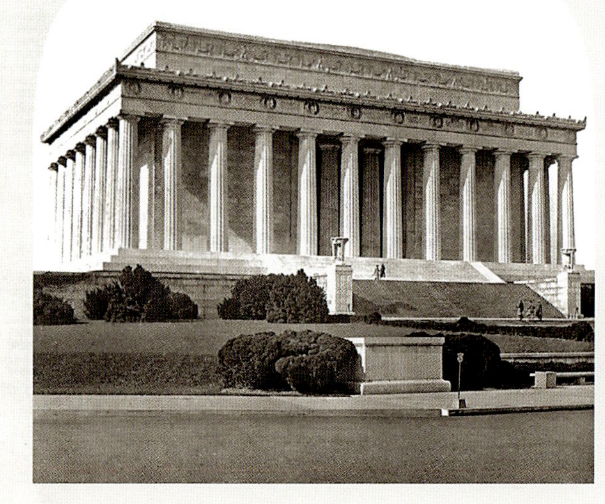

The Lincoln Memorial

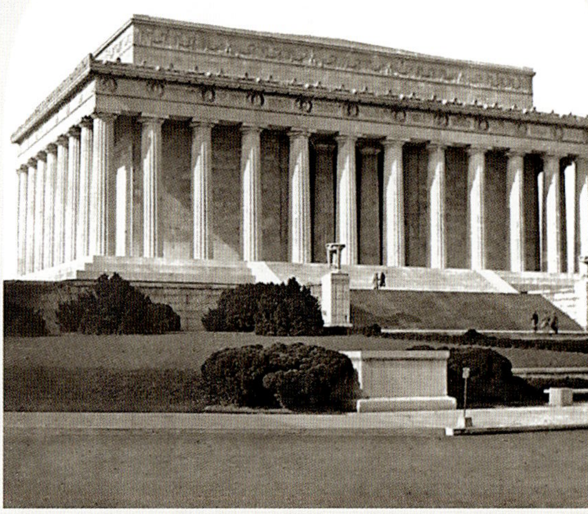

The Lincoln Memorial

The Great Statue in the Lincoln Memorial

Inside the Lincoln Memorial is the colossal seated figure of Abraham Lincoln, by the sculptor Daniel Chester French. At the turn of the century, French was the premier American sculptor. French was chosen by Henry Bacon, the monument's architect. For his studies, French viewed the photographs of Lincoln made by Mathew Brady. The impressive sculpture is made of twenty-eight pieces of white Georgia marble, weighing 170 tons. The inscription above Lincoln's head states: *In this temple as in the hearts of the people for whom he saved the Union the memory of Abraham Lincoln is enshrined forever.*

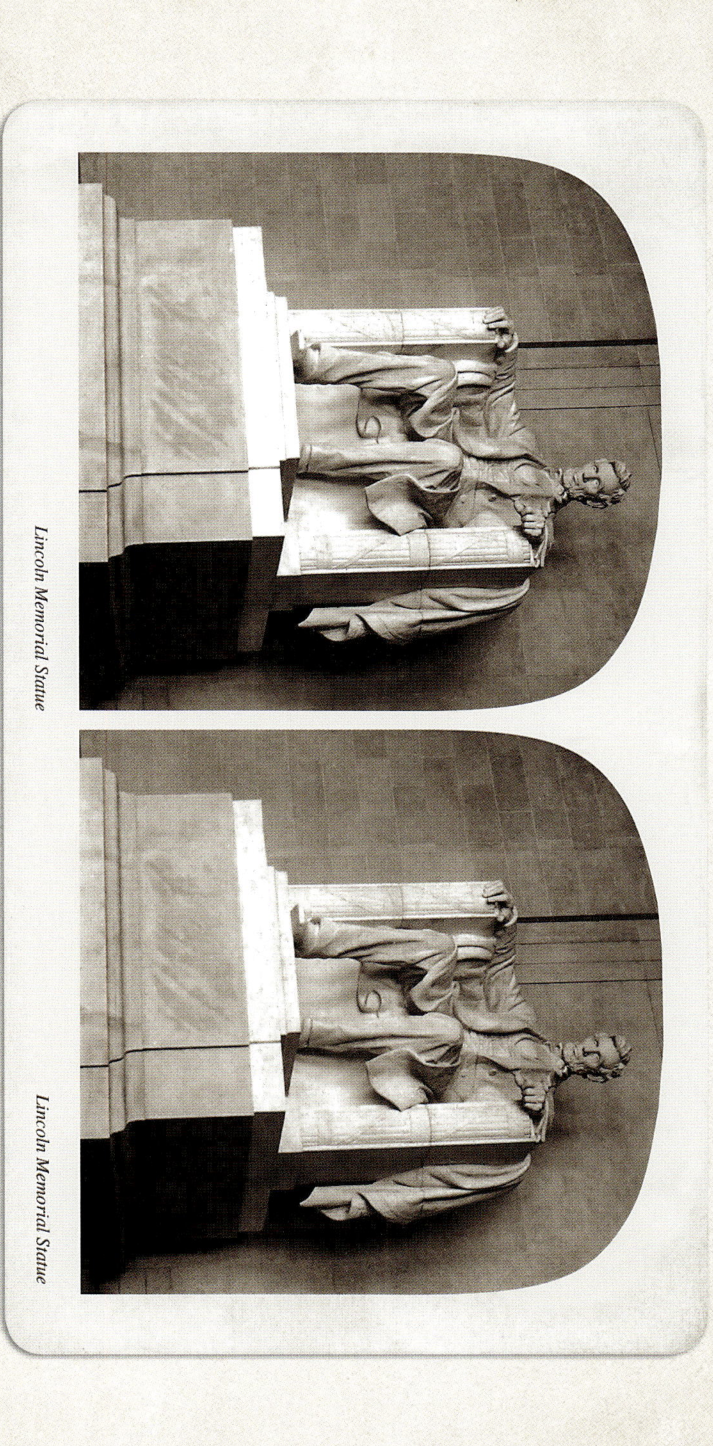
Lincoln Memorial Statue
Lincoln Memorial Statue

General Robert E. Lee's Old Home, Arlington, Virginia

General (then Colonel) Lee was living in this Greek temple-style house when the Civil War broke out, and he felt that duty called him to cast his lot with the state rather than the federal Union. Early in the course of the long struggle between North and South, federal troops took possession of the estate. In 1864, Arlington National Cemetery was established on the grounds. Sometime after the close of the war, a son of General Lee brought a claim against the federal government for the estate, and the Supreme Court granted the claim. But he consented to the sale of the property to the government and since 1883 it has belonged to the United States.

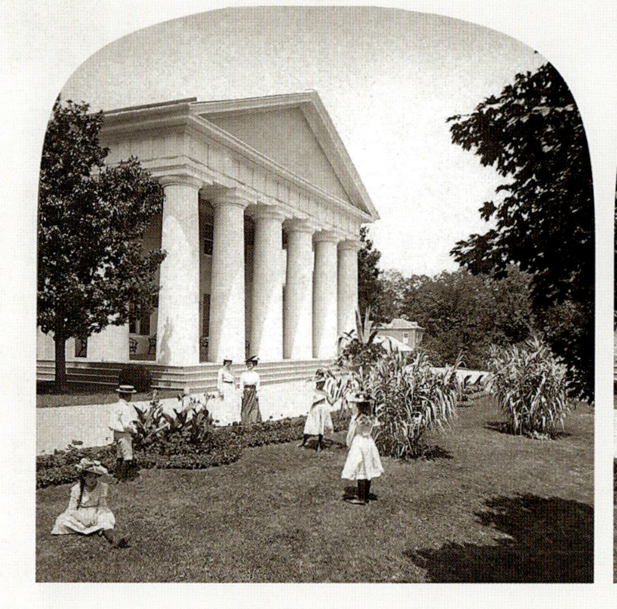

Home of Robert E. Lee, Arlington

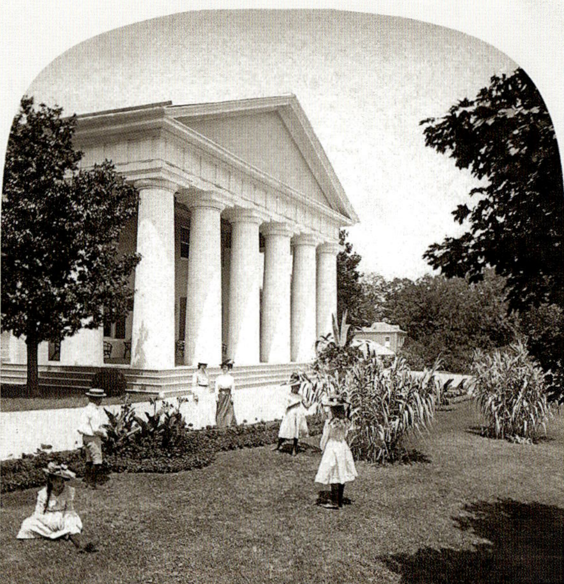

Home of Robert E. Lee, Arlington

On the Way to the Inauguration

Pedestrians along the avenue and others in carriages are on their way to the inauguration of Benjamin Harrison in 1889. The buildings and street life of the city appear along Washington's wide streets with advertisements for H. F. Woodward, men's furnishings, and W. S. Thompson, a well-known druggist. Benjamin Harrison served as president from 1889 to 1893. Grover Cleveland served as president before Harrison, and defeated him in the election of 1892.

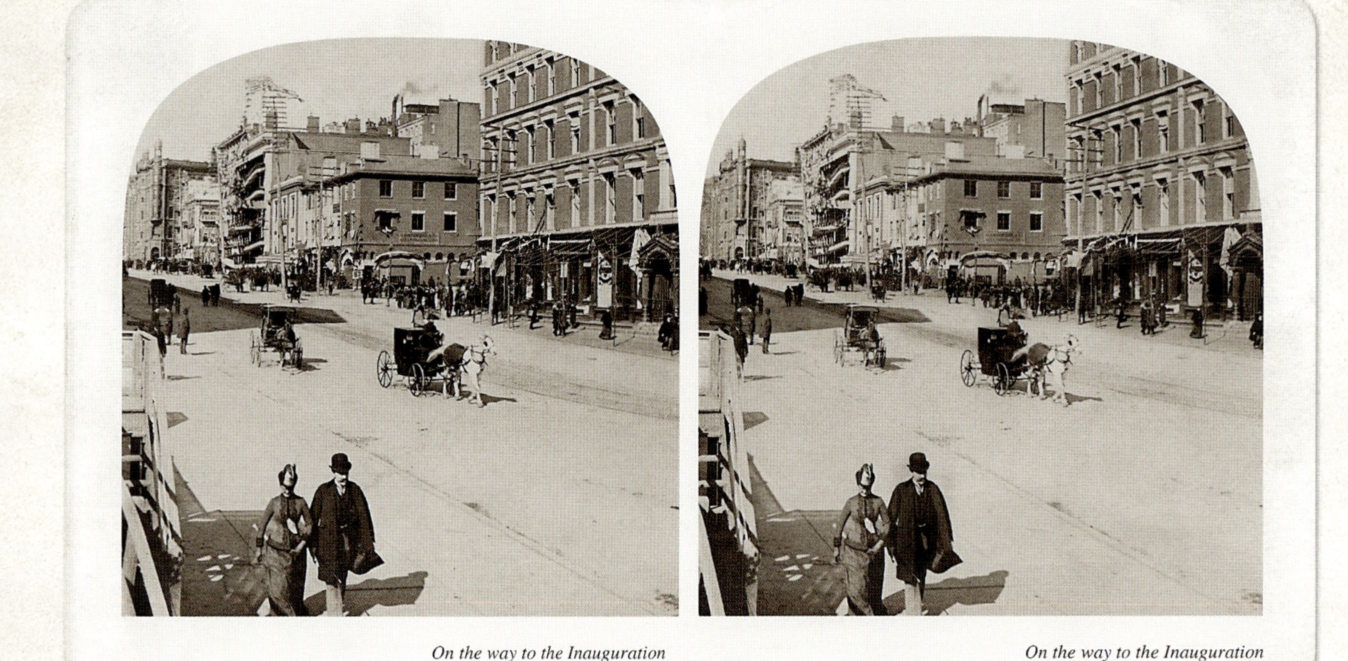

On the way to the Inauguration

On the way to the Inauguration

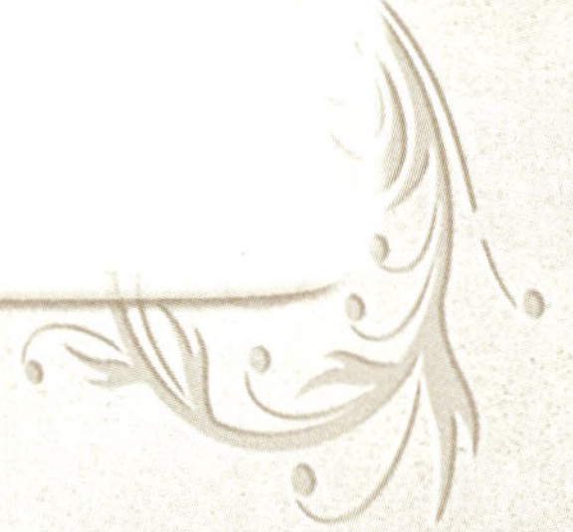

Grover Cleveland and Adlai Stevenson

Grover Cleveland is the only president to serve two non-consecutive terms. From 1885 to 1889, Cleveland was elected with Thomas A. Hendricks as vice president. The following term Cleveland was defeated by Benjamin Harrison. Cleveland won re-election in 1893 with Adlai Stevenson serving as his vice president. Cleveland's work as a lawyer in New York State had earned him a reputation for honesty and common sense. As Cleveland and Stevenson parade along the expanse of Pennsylvania Avenue, crowds of observers line the streets and perch on its buildings.

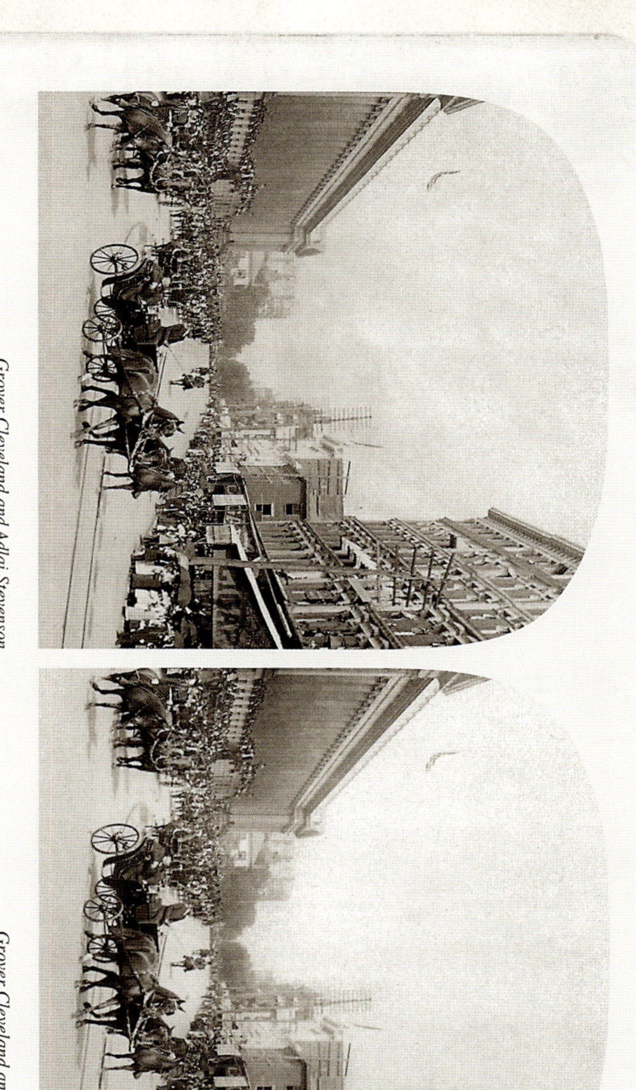
Grover Cleveland and Adlai Stevenson
Grover Cleveland and Adlai Stevenson

Pennsylvania Avenue from the Treasury, Southeast to the United States Capitol

The Capitol is viewed from the entrance to the Treasury Building looking along Pennsylvania Avenue. While the Capitol appears to be only a few blocks in the distance, it is actually a little over a mile away. The broad avenue, seen with carriages and streetcars, is the scene of official parades and processions. It was one of the first streets built in Washington and dates from the late eighteenth century. Thomas Jefferson and George Washington agreed that it should be Washington's "Grand Avenue" and the former had the route planted with fast growing Lombardy poplars to emphasize its importance. Since Jefferson's second inauguration, every president of the United States has ceremonially paraded down Pennsylvania Avenue after taking the oath of office.

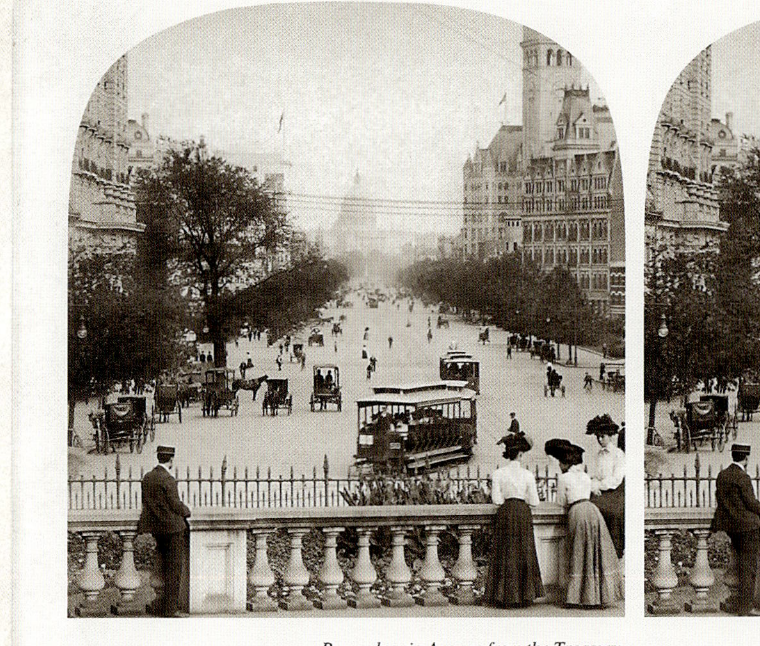

Pennsylvania Avenue from the Treasury

Pennsylvania Avenue from the Treasury

The Capitol

The soaring, graceful dome of the Capitol, seen against the sky and in reflection, rises over 180 feet in height from the floor of the rotunda to the interior of the canopy. Its proportions are so admirable that in spite of its great size, it conveys an impression of uplifting lightness rather than ponderous weight. The Capitol is sited on Jenkins Hill and was designed as part of the city plan that also included the grand boulevard—later called Pennsylvania Avenue—which linked it to the President's House—later called the White House. In 1791, Pierre L'Enfant, a French artist and engineer, designed the city plans for Washington, D.C. He designated the location of the Capitol building and the Executive Mansion, and outlined the main thoroughfare, Pennsylvania Avenue, to connect the two. His plan specified grand, tree-lined avenues. Four avenues radiate from Capitol Hill, the center of America's government, dividing Washington into four quarters.

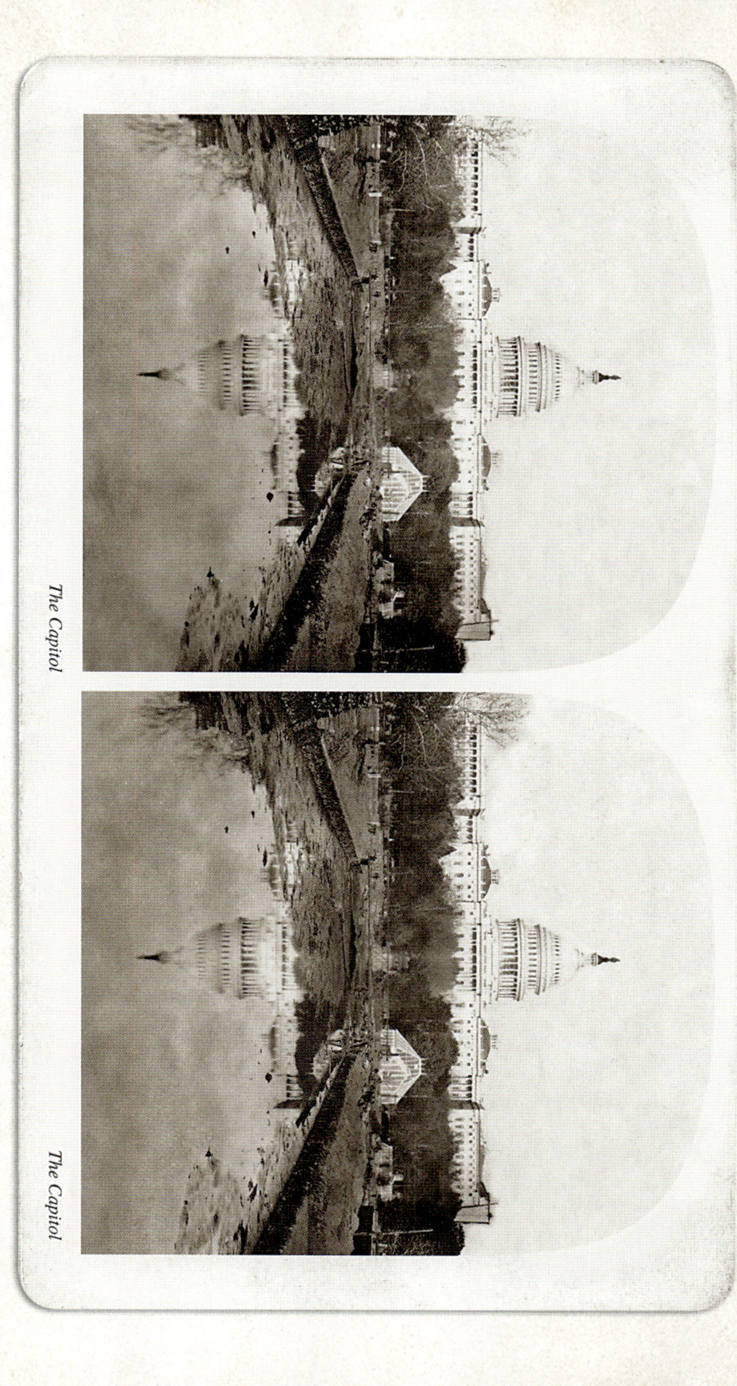

The Capitol

The Capitol

Visitors to the Capitol

The building of the Capitol extended over several presidencies; the Senate wing was completed by 1800 and the first session of Congress was held in the incomplete building that November 17. The House wing was completed by 1811, but a fire during the War of 1812 left the building severely damaged and requiring extensive and long restoration. Reconstruction started in 1815 and although completed four years later work intermittently continued on the building as a whole until the first dome was finished in 1864. However meanwhile the number of congressmen had increased from new states and by 1850 the building was no longer of adequate size to accommodate them. Architect Thomas U. Walter was selected and the construction of new wings began in 1851.

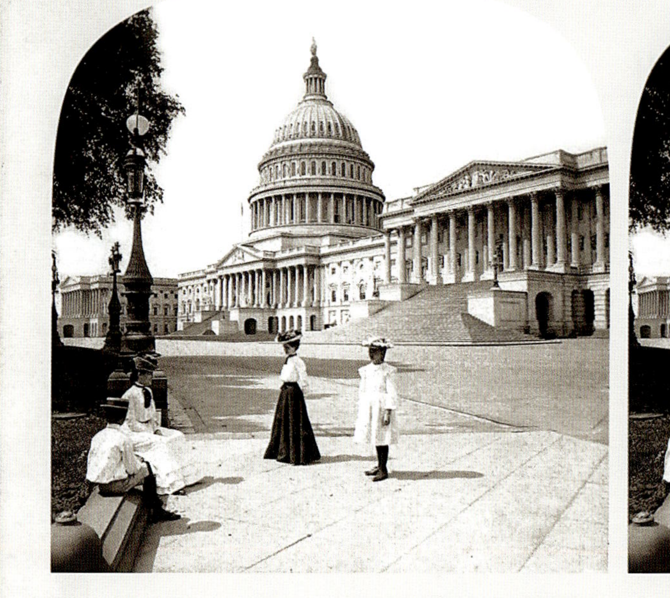
Visitors to the Capitol

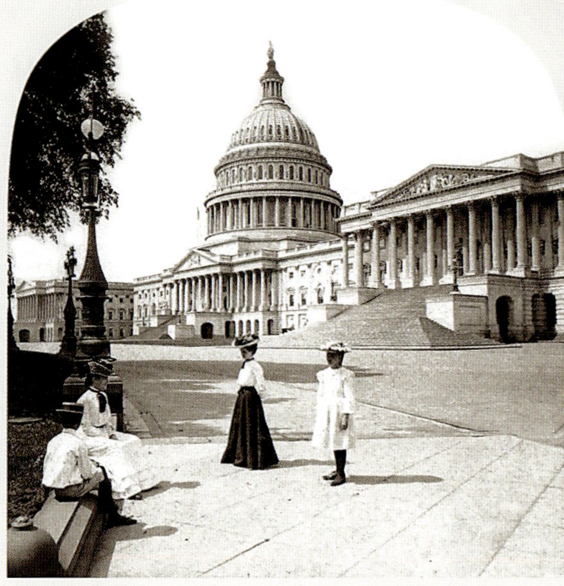
Visitors to the Capitol

The Capitol

The Capitol is the highest architectural expression of America's national spirit. Before it was built the U.S. Congress usually convened in Philadelphia, but after an angry mob attacked the Congress there, the senators wanted a new location. Many cities wanted the prestige of being the permanent capital and Washington was only agreed on as part of a compromise involving the payment of debts incurred during the Revolutionary War. The Capitol's cornerstone was laid by George Washington on September 18, 1793. The original design, by Dr. William Thornton, presented a building composed of three sections, the central dome flanked by two wings on either side for the Senate and House of Representatives. It was built at a cost of $412,000. The structure as it now stands embodies the concepts of several architects and the work of several generations.

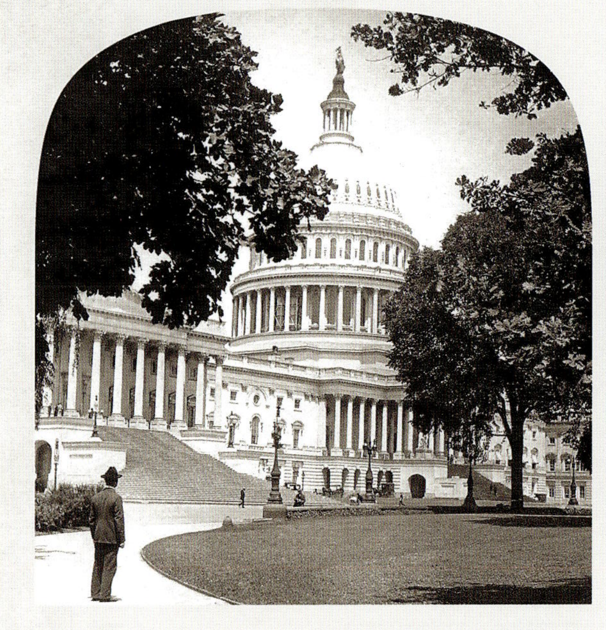

The United States Capitol

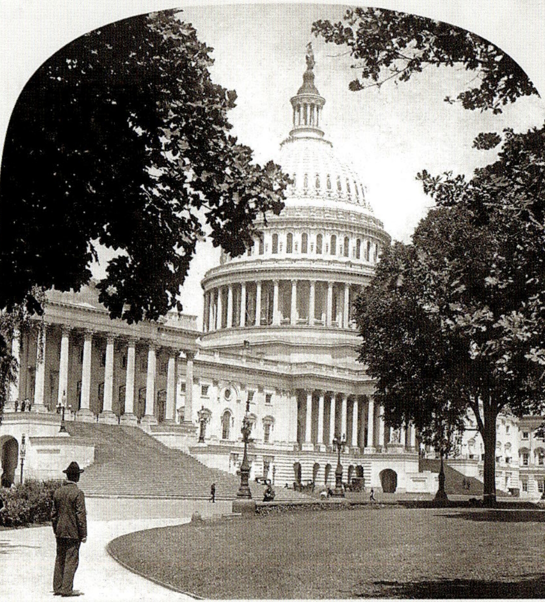

The United States Capitol

Bird's-Eye View of Washington

Looking past the south portico of the White House, the sites and buildings of the nation's capital are seen into the horizon. With the dome of the Capitol and the Treasury Building in the background, Pierre L'Enfant's city planning for Washington, D.C. appears to great effect with its greenery and generous avenues leading to the city's monuments.

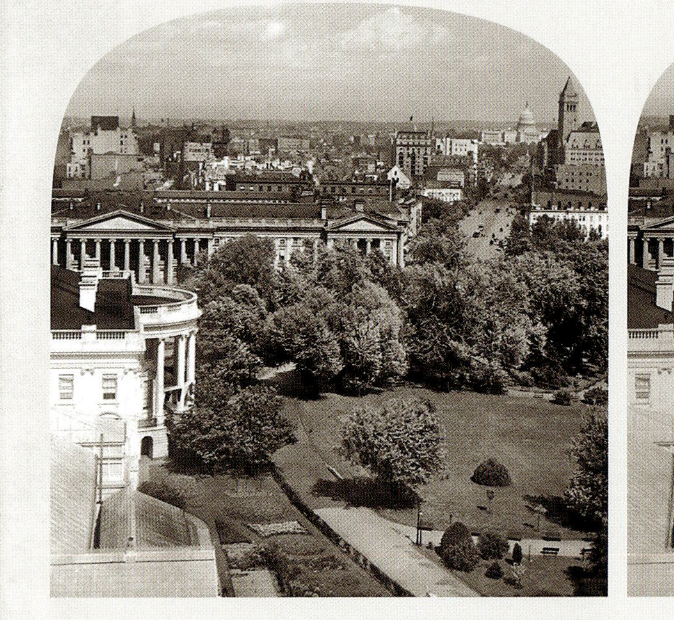

The White House to the Capitol

The White House to the Capitol

Southeast to the White House

One of the high windows on the eastern side of the State, War, and Navy Building provides this view of the Executive Mansion and grounds. The cornerstone was laid in 1792 in the presence of George Washington, but the Executive Mansion was first occupied in 1800 when President John Quincy Adams and his wife moved into the still unfinished home. The original building was badly damaged in 1814, when it was burned by the British. When repairs were completed, the freestone walls were painted white to conceal damage done by the fire, and this led to the name "White House," by which it was popularly known for many years before the phrase was given official acceptance by Theodore Roosevelt in 1901.

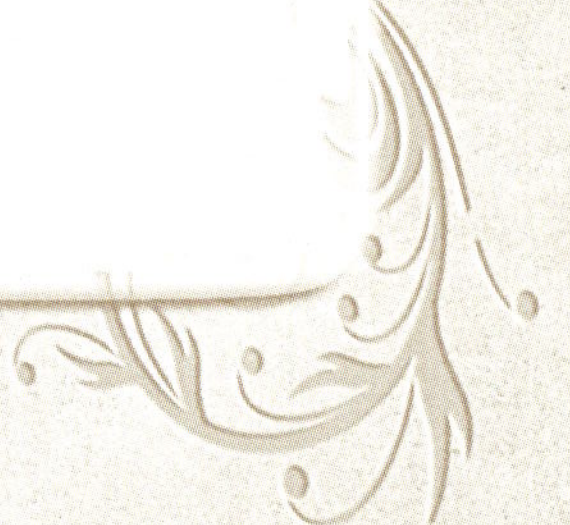

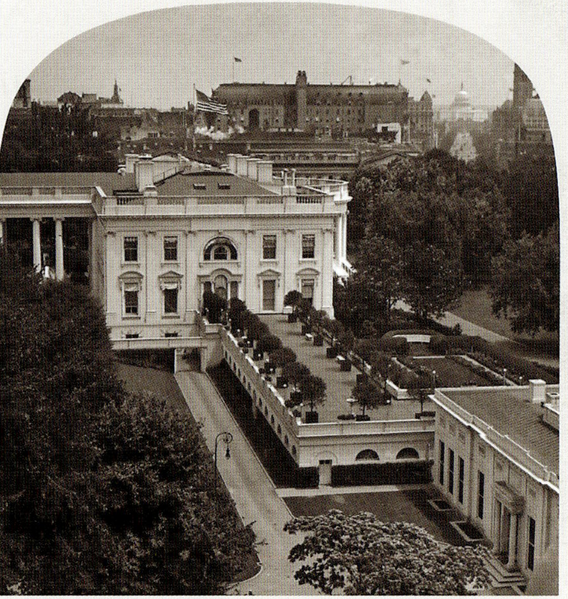

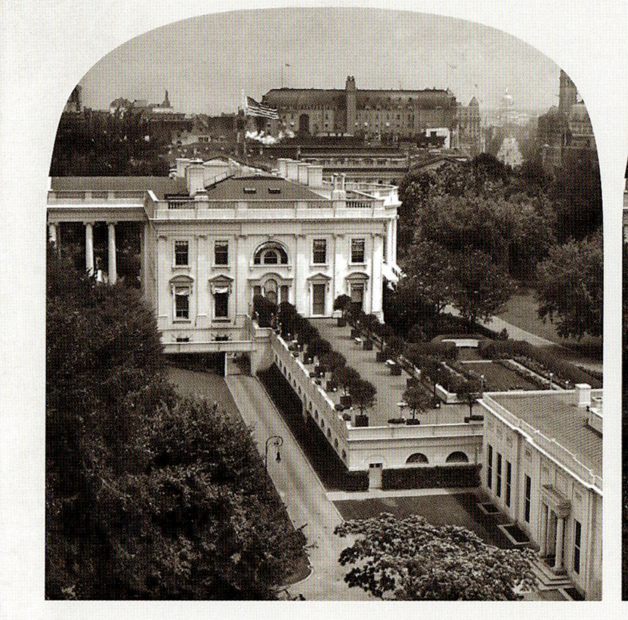

Southeast to the Capitol, past the White House

Southeast to the Capitol, past the White House

The White House

The White House, home of presidents and their families, is the oldest structure in Washington devoted to public use. The site of the President's House, now 1600 Pennsylvania Avenue, was selected by George Washington with city planner Pierre L'Enfant. A competition was held, nine proposals were submitted, and James Hoban, an Irish-born architect, was selected as the winning designer. A symbol of the United States, the White House contains over one hundred rooms, including the magnificent East Room. Its diverse uses have included drying the laundry of Abigail Adams, weddings of presidential family members, and receptions of foreign rulers and potentates.

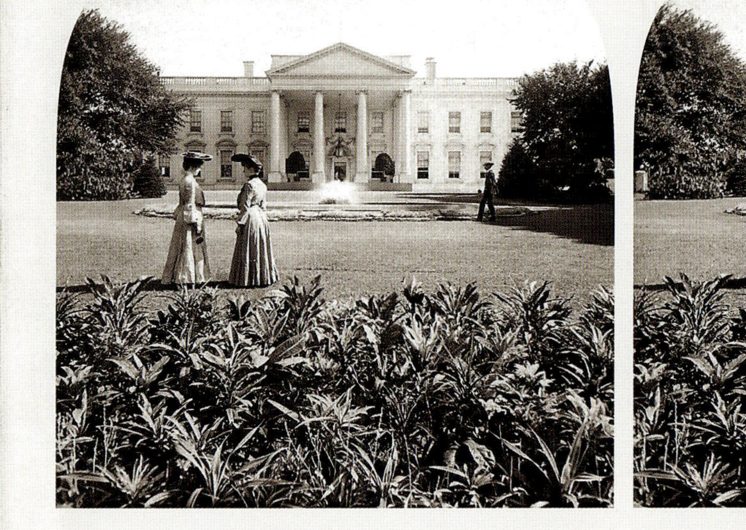

The White House

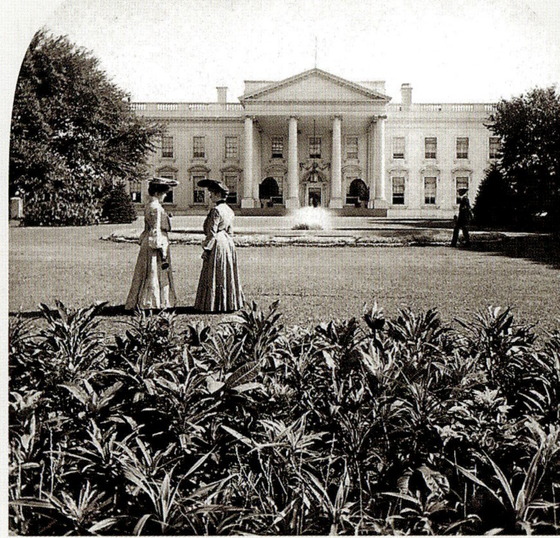

The White House

President Roosevelt Signing Bills

Roosevelt's first American ancestors came to America from Holland in 1640. Born October 27, 1858 in New York City, Roosevelt became a member of the New York State Assembly in 1882. In 1886 he was Republican candidate for mayor of New York City but was defeated. After serving on the U.S. Civil Service Commission, Roosevelt worked as president of the Board of Police Commissioners of New York City from 1895 to 1897. Roosevelt then became Assistant Secretary of the Navy, a post he resigned for duty in the Spanish War. From 1899 to 1900 Roosevelt served as governor of New York and then became vice president in 1900. On the death of President McKinley on September 14, 1901, Roosevelt became the twenty-sixth president of the United States.

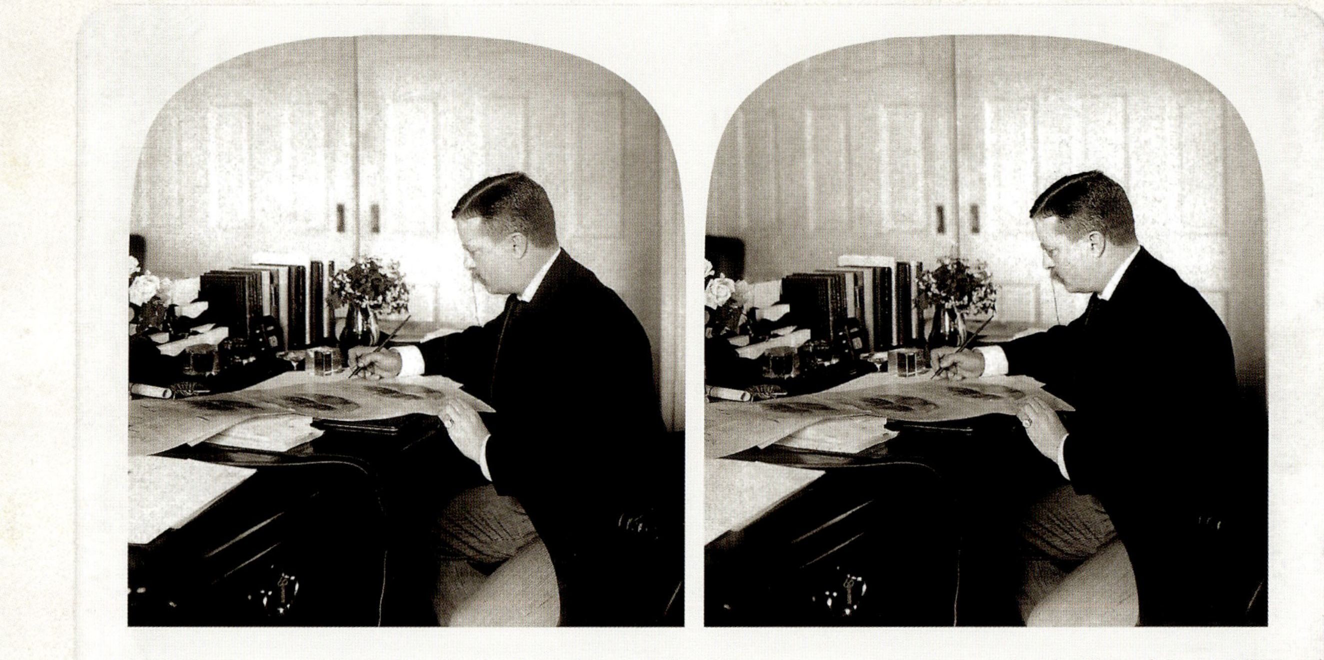

President Roosevelt Signing Bills President Roosevelt Signing Bills

The President's Office

The president's office in the White House displays a formal room with a marble fireplace, gas chandelier, and spittoons. A large table, with three sets of pens, ink, and blotters, is set for important presidential business. On the wall can be seen a map of the world. When the Oval Office was created in 1909 as part of an expansion of the West Wing, it became the official office of the president.

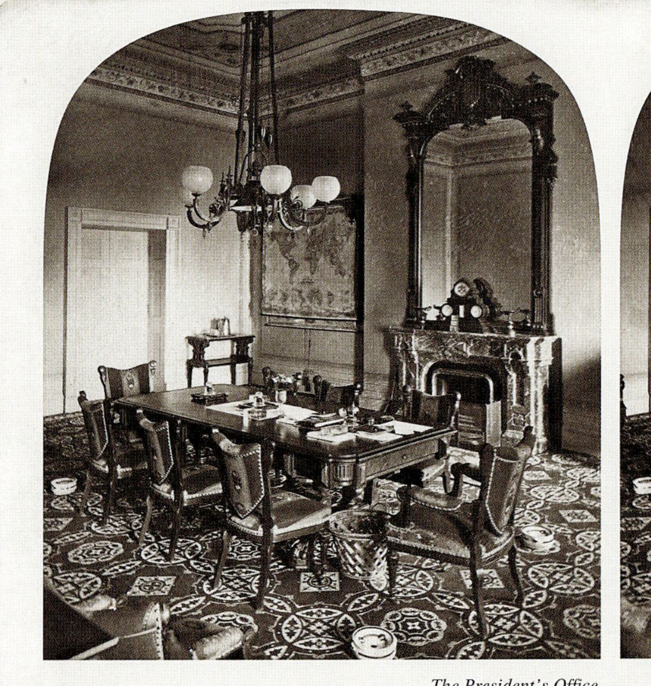

The President's Office

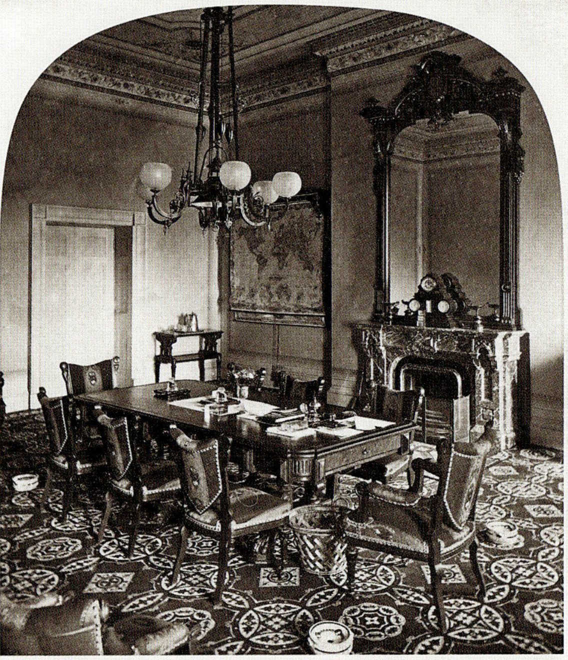

The President's Office

The President's Library, White House

The numerous rooms of the Executive Mansion were used in various fashions by the presidents and their families. The President's Library is a large, pleasant room on the ground floor and is decorated in comfortable style with floral wallpaper, a wicker seat, and striped upholstery on chairs and a chaise lounge. Abigail Adams is credited with forming the first library in the White House in the room her husband, President John Adams, originally used as a laundry. Mrs. McKinley used this room to receive close family friends.

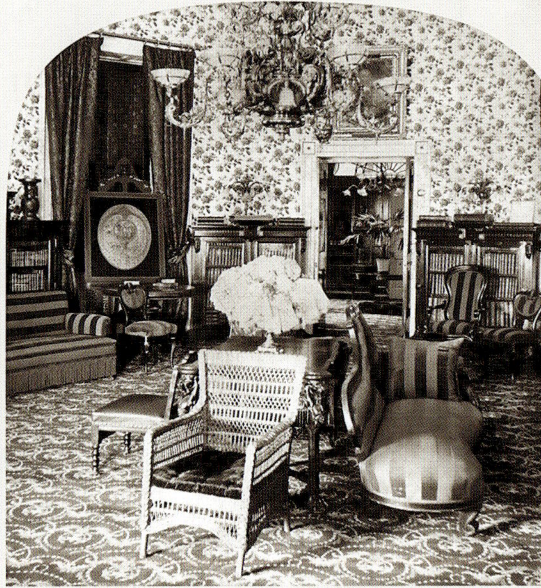

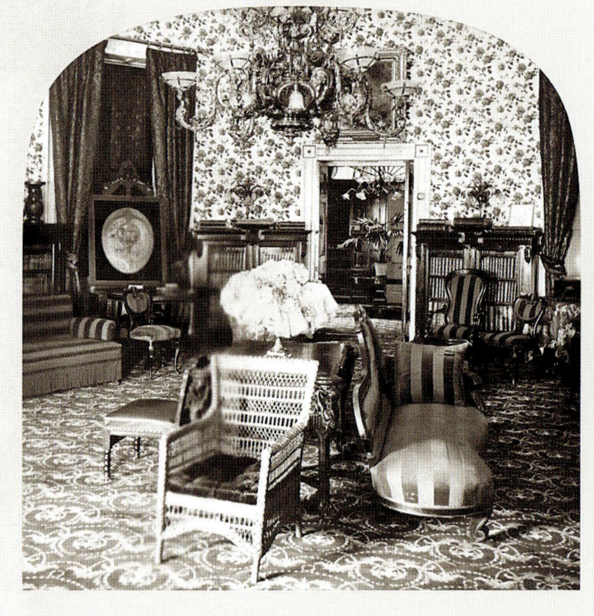

The President's Library

The President's Library

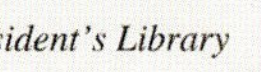

Sioux and Crow Chiefs at the White House

In 1820, a Senate resolution established the Senate Committee on Indian Affairs to address matters relating to Indians. Plenty Coos, Chief of the Crow Nation, seen here arriving at the White House to visit President Harding, testified often in the early twentieth century before Congressional committees regarding issues relating to his people. Chief Plenty Coos was also among those who participated in the dedication of the Tomb of the Unknown Soldier in Arlington Cemetery in 1921. Representing the nation's Indians, he laid his war bonnet on the tomb as a tribute to all the Indian tribes and nations.

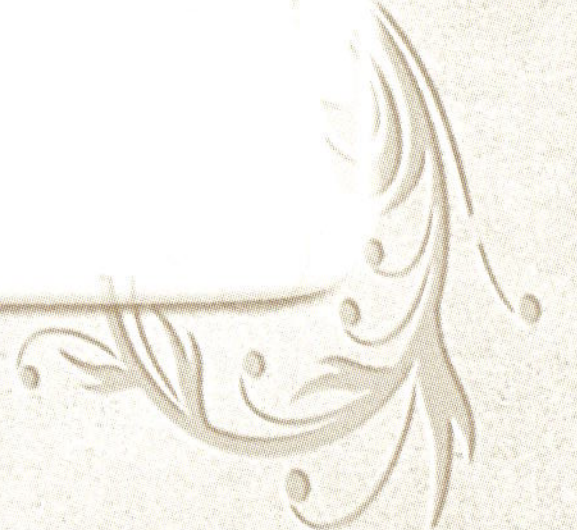

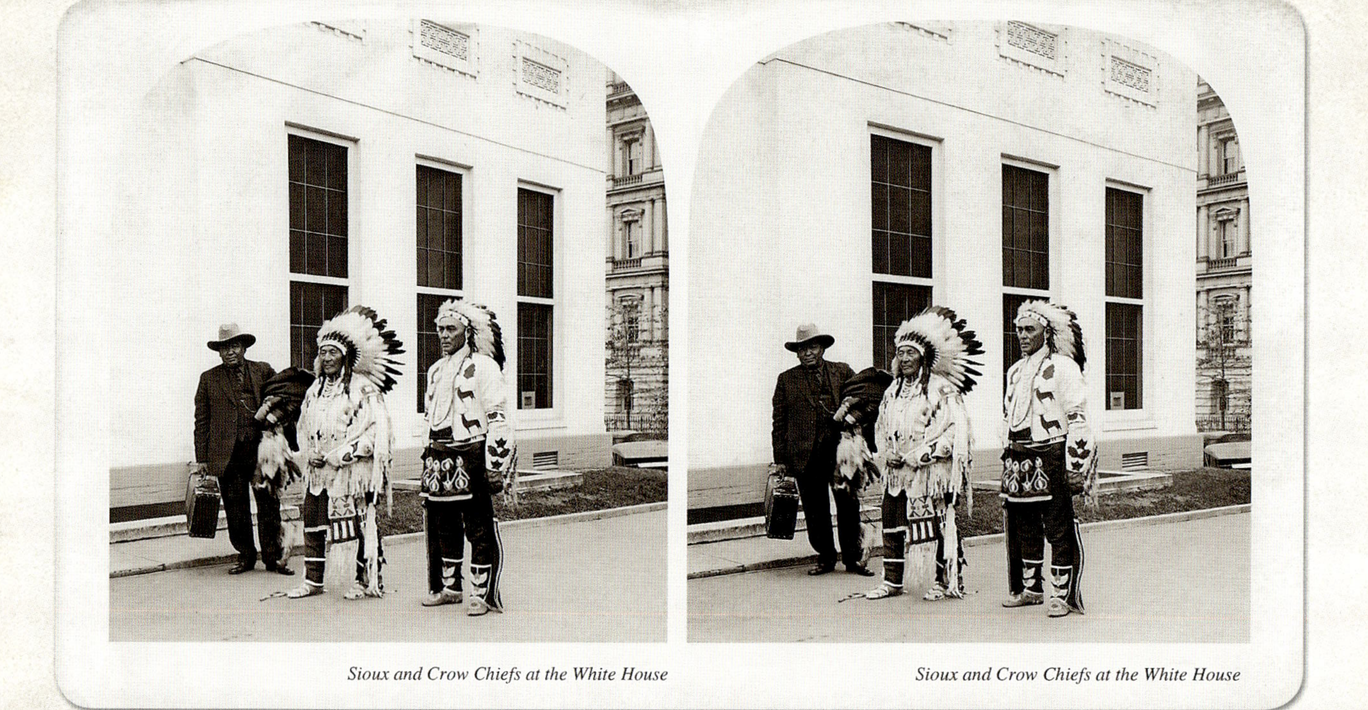

Sioux and Crow Chiefs at the White House

Sioux and Crow Chiefs at the White House

President Roosevelt's Dinner for Prince Henry

On February 24, 1902, Prince Henry of Prussia, brother of the German emperor, was a distinguished guest at the White House. The prince was received by President Roosevelt in the Blue Parlor, where the prince introduced himself to the president since there was no one in Washington of high enough rank to make a formal introduction. Prince Henry was then led by Roosevelt to the Green Room, where the prince met the rest of Roosevelt's family. That evening a dinner was given for Prince Henry, with the banquet taking place in the East Room, instead of the State Dining Room, to accommodate the large number of guests. Thousands of tiny electric lights decorated the room, some in the form of naval motifs including anchors, ropes, and stars.

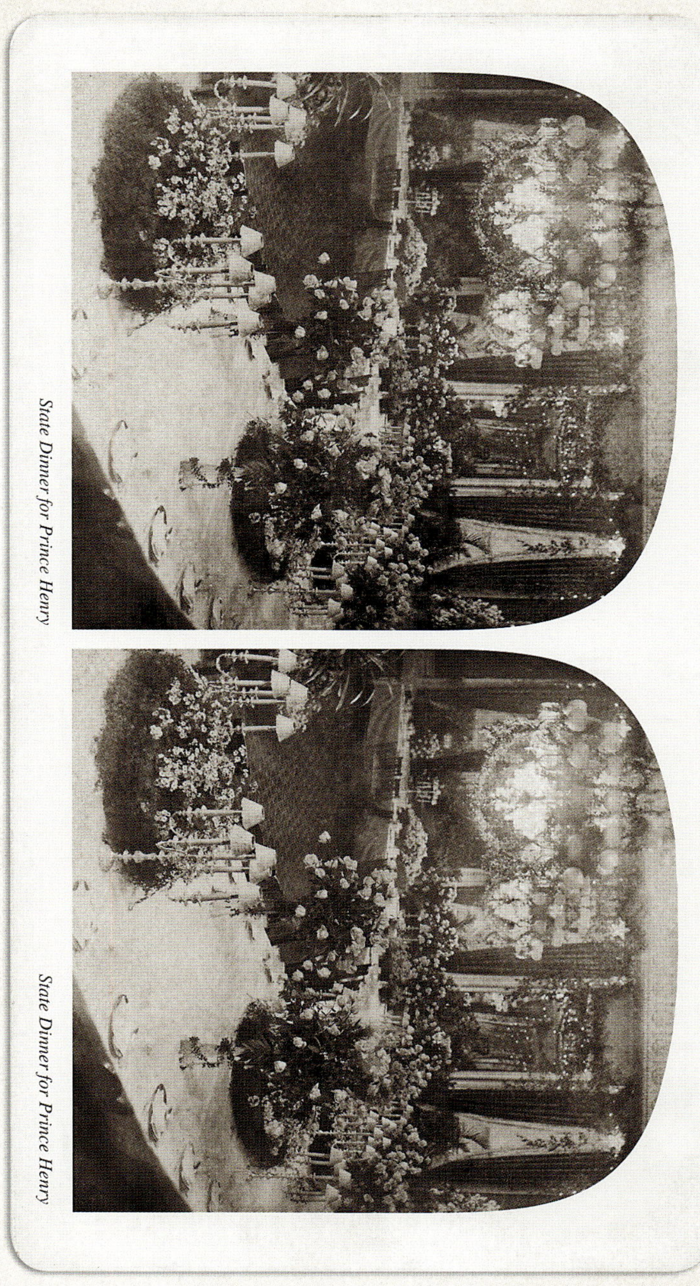

State Dinner for Prince Henry

State Dinner for Prince Henry

Easter Morning in the White House

Most of the holidays observed by Americans are celebrated in the White House. Rooms are decorated and often dinners and receptions are held. When there are children in the First Family, White House holidays can be very lively. For Easter, a marble topped sideboard features a display of Easter lilies and ferns, as well as a large confectionery egg decorated with roses and an inscription of "Easter Greetings."

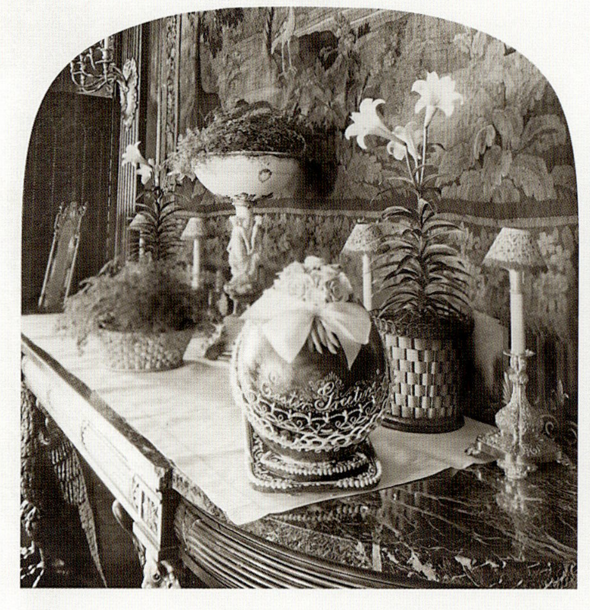

Easter Morning in the White House

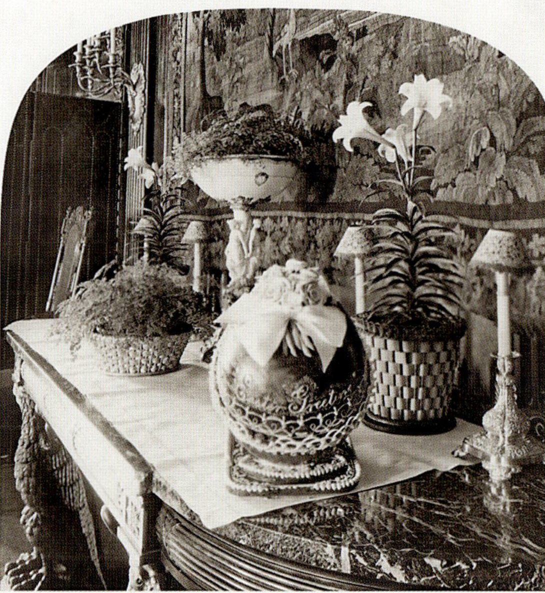

Easter Morning in the White House

Easter Monday Egg Roll at the White House

The Easter Monday egg rolling tradition in Washington, D.C. began in the 1870s on the grounds of the U.S. Capitol. Along with rolling dyed eggs down a hill, games such as "Egg Ball" and "Egg Croquet" were also played. Concern for the lawn led to a bill banning such uses at the Capitol, and in 1876 President Ulysses S. Grant signed the bill into law. The ban caused great disappointment to the children from all levels of Washington society who attended the Easter egg party. It was President Rutherford B. Hayes, in 1878, who invited children to use the White House lawn for the Easter egg roll, establishing it as an annual White House event.

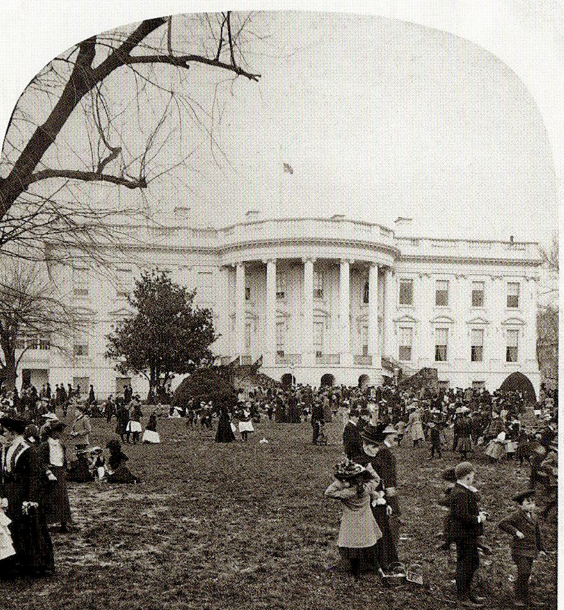

Easter Monday Egg Roll at the White House

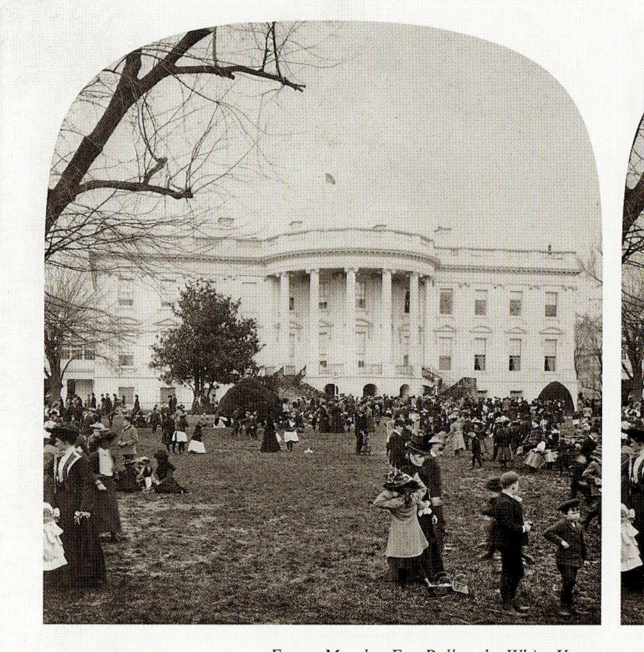

Easter Monday Egg Roll at the White House

Library of Congress

The Library of Congress is America's great free national library. The building of the monumental structure for the Library was begun in 1889 and completed in 1897. The magnificent Library faces exactly west, sitting on approximately ten acres of land. Its exterior is made of granite quarried in Concord, New Hampshire, while marble from all over the world is used in the interior. It is 470 feet long (from north to south), and 340 feet deep (from west to east).

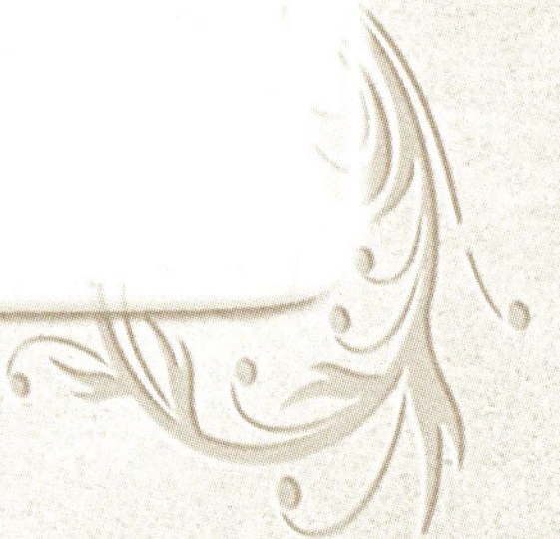

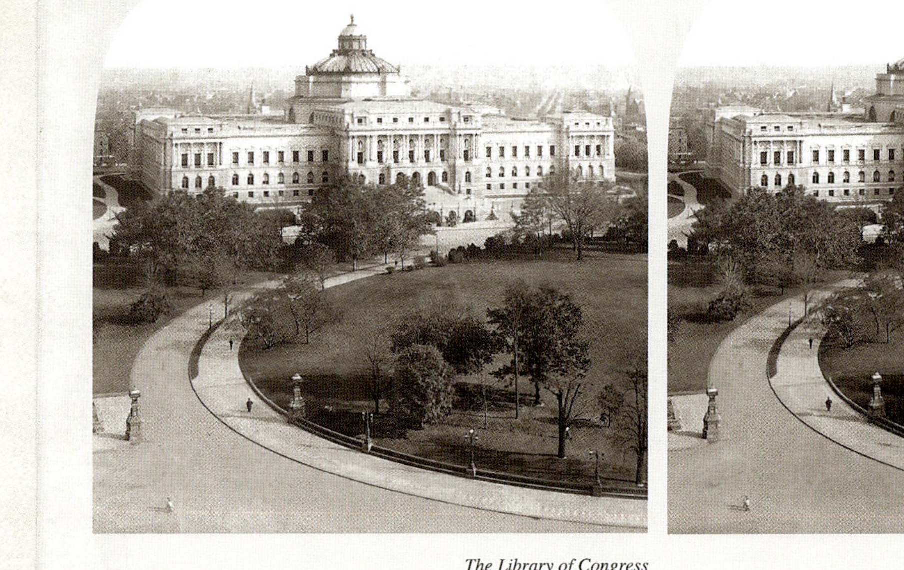
The Library of Congress
The Library of Congress

Grand Staircase, Library of Congress

This northern staircase (there is a similar staircase on the south side) presents the magnificence of the Library. The arch of Italian marble seen here leads to the vast, high-walled Reading Room in the center of the building, under the dome. Red Italian marbles inlaid in the hall floor come from Verona and yellow slabs are from Siena. The eight-foot bronze figure holding a torch of lights is by Philip Martiny. Along the railing of the staircase there are sculptures in high relief of children representing occupations and pursuits including a gardener, an entomologist, a student, a printer, a musician, and a physician. Behind the room's many arches are mural paintings such as Charles Sprague Pearce's series depicting *Religion, Labor, Study*, and *Recreation*.

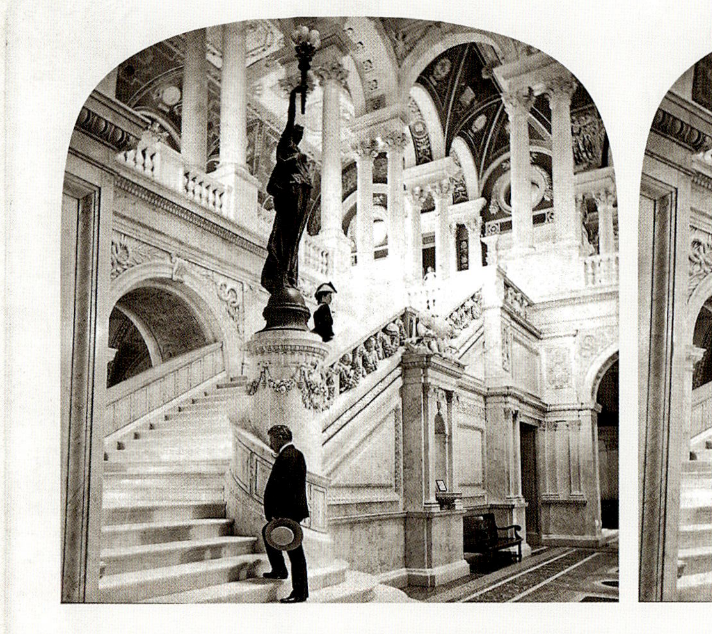

Grand Staircase, Library of Congress

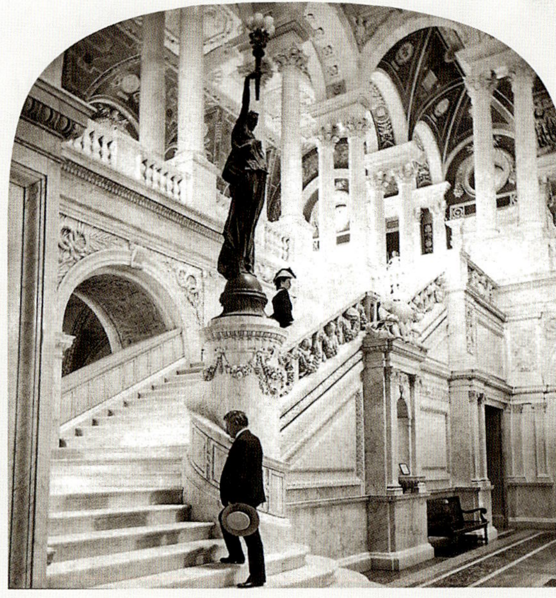

Grand Staircase, Library of Congress

Congressional Library in the Capitol

The collections of the original Library of Congress, founded in 1800, were housed in the Capitol until a fire set by British troops in 1814 burned the building. Then for $23,950 Congress bought Thomas Jefferson's library, consisting of approximately 6,700 volumes that he had collected over some fifty years, to form a second collection but it too was largely lost to fire in December 1851. The following year Congress appropriated funds of $168,000 to purchase books to replace those destroyed but not to add new works. The Library of Congress started expanding after 1865 and acquired the huge libraries of the Smithsonian and the huge numbers of books belonging to historian Peter Force. By 1876 the Library had around 300,000 volumes. In 1897 the Library moved away from the Capitol into its new home in Washington, by which time the collection had expanded to around 840,000 volumes. It has continued to grow ever since.

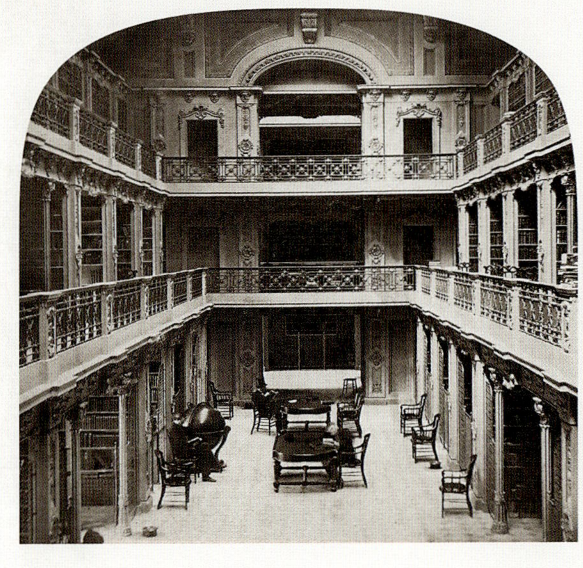

The Congressional Library

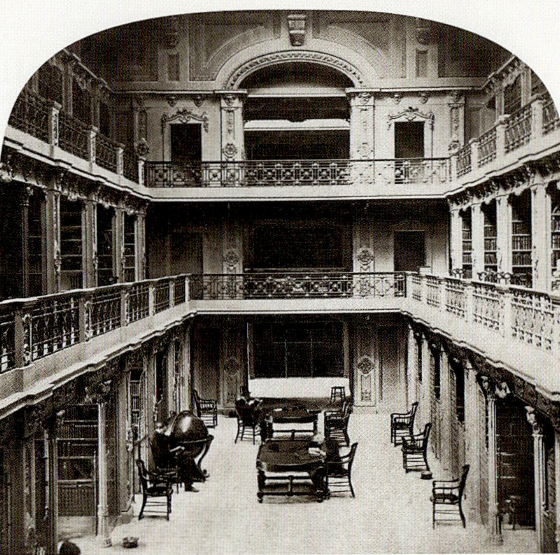

The Congressional Library

Skeleton Room, National Museum

The United States National Museum building opened in 1881. Visitors from throughout the world came to see the museum's wonderful collections. The National Museum, part of the Smithsonian, which was created in 1846 with a bequest from James Smithson, housed many of the museum's exhibitions of history, natural history, animals, geology, and art. Displays such as the Skeleton Room were favorite places for children to discover natural history as they viewed the skeletons seen in cases and suspended from above.

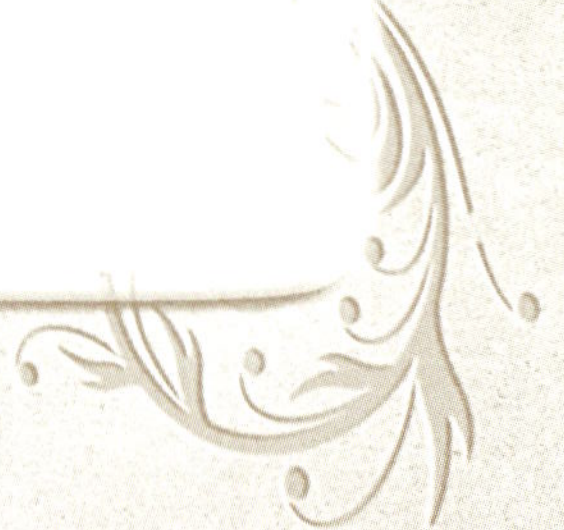

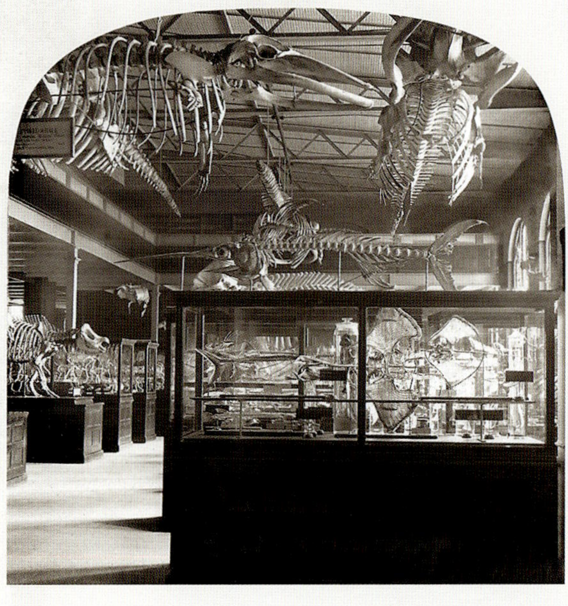
Smithsonian Skeleton Room

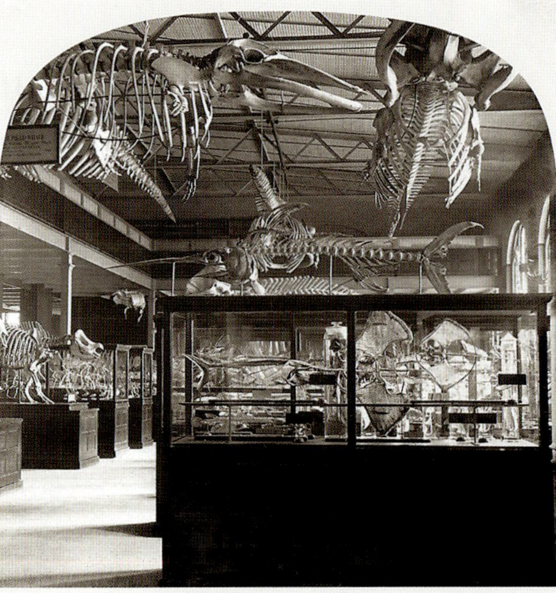
Smithsonian Skeleton Room

Machines for Casting Type for Printing, Bureau of Engraving and Printing

In 1862, the Bureau of Engraving and Printing began in one room in the basement of the Treasury Building with two men and four women sorting out $1 and $2 bills printed by private companies. The previous year, with concern about counterfeiting during the Civil War, Congress had authorized the federal government to begin issuing paper money. In 1874, legislation was passed to officially recognize the Bureau of Engraving and Printing. Along with paper currency, the Bureau of Engraving and Printing also began producing the country's postage stamps in 1894. Most employees in the Bureau came under civil service jurisdiction in 1888 and by 1908 all the jobs within the Bureau were government positions.

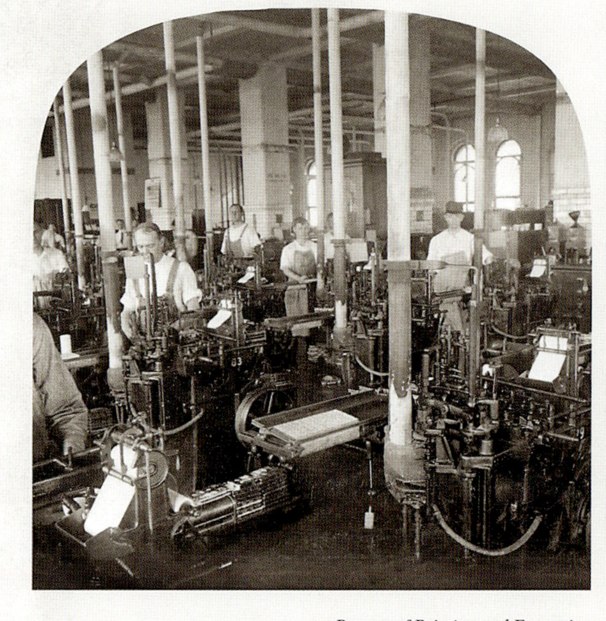

Bureau of Printing and Engraving

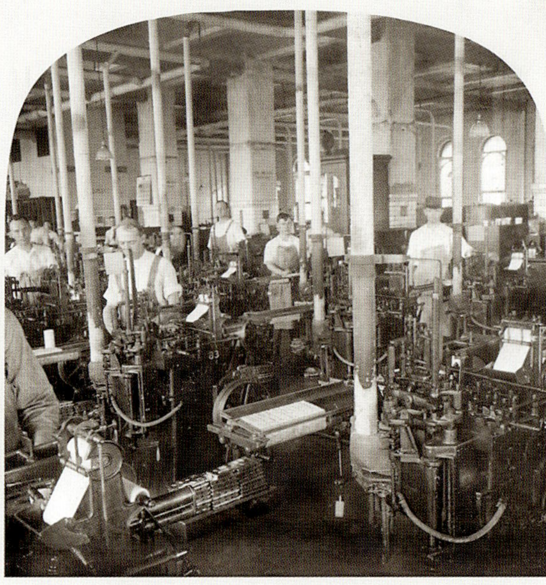

Bureau of Printing and Engraving

Engraving the Plates for Printing Paper Money, Bureau of Engraving and Printing

These men are preparing engraved plates used to print United States paper currency to go into the Federal Reserve. Coins are produced by the U.S. Mint. Money issued by the government was printed by private bank note companies during the first century of the new country's existence, but by 1877 all United States currency was produced by the Bureau. The first dollar bills were issued by the federal government in 1862 at which time they showed a portrait of Salmon P. Chase, the Secretary of the Treasury; seven years later the portrait of George Washington was added. The $2 bill also first appeared in 1862 but sported the portrait of Alexander Hamilton, the first Secretary of the Treasury; seven years later the portrait of Thomas Jefferson was added.

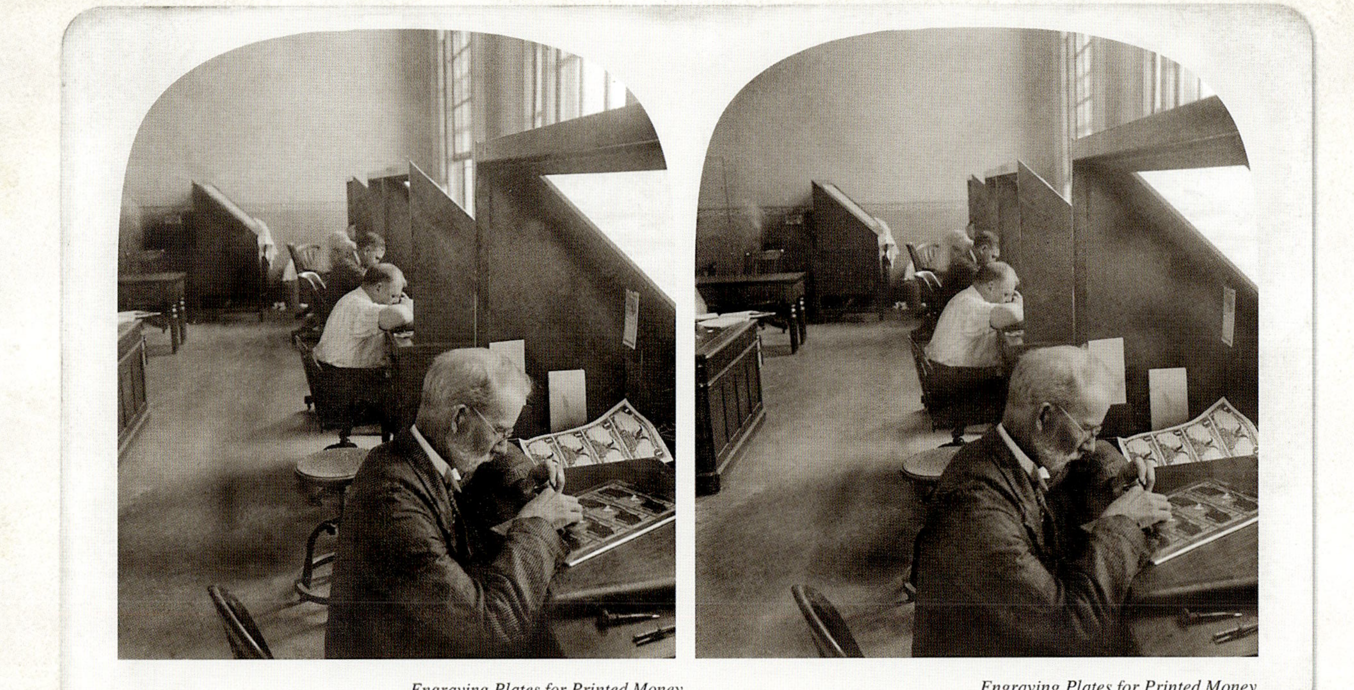

Engraving Plates for Printed Money

Engraving Plates for Printed Money

14th Street Circle

The center of the 14th Street Circle, at the intersection of Massachusetts and Vermont Avenues and 14th and M Streets N.W., stands the equestrian statue of Major-General George H. Thomas. The statue was erected in 1879. This view was taken from the Portland Flats, on the south side of the circle. Portland Flats, designed by architect Adolph Cluss, was the first luxury apartment building in Washington. Memorial Evangelical Lutheran Church, built in 1873, appears across the circle. A statue of Martin Luther stands in front of the church.

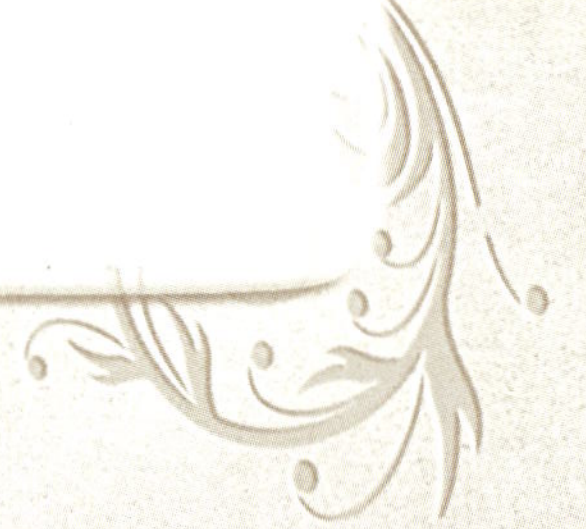

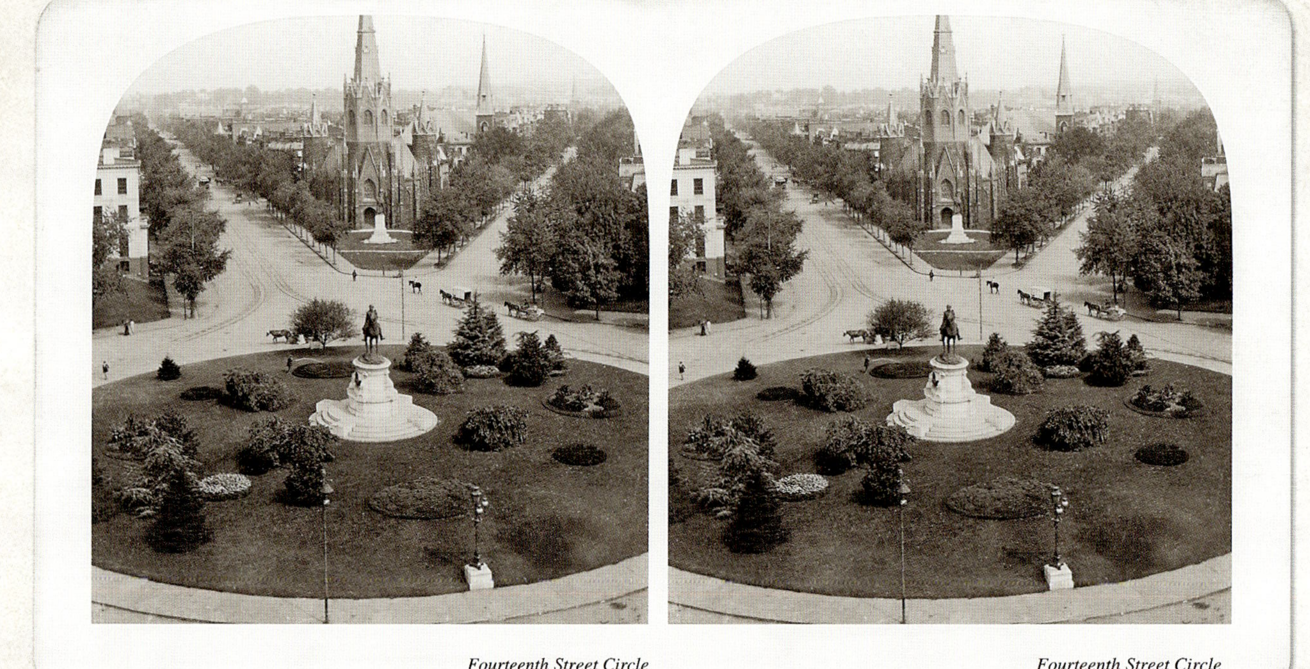

Fourteenth Street Circle

Fourteenth Street Circle

President McKinley delivering his Inaugural Address, March 4, 1897

In 1896, William McKinley, a Republican congressman from Ohio, won the presidential election over William Jennings Bryan to become the twenty-fifth president of the United States. McKinley took the oath of office from a platform on the front steps of the Capitol. The oath was administered by Chief Justice Melville Fuller. In his Inaugural Address, McKinley called for revisions to the financial system, observations of severe economy in all public expenditures, and the following of a firm and dignified foreign policy. McKinley's inauguration was the first to be filmed by Thomas Edison's new motion picture camera.

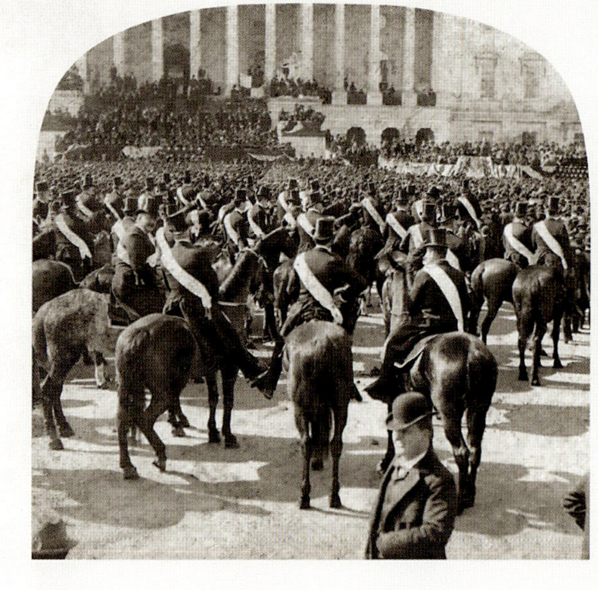

Inauguration of President McKinley

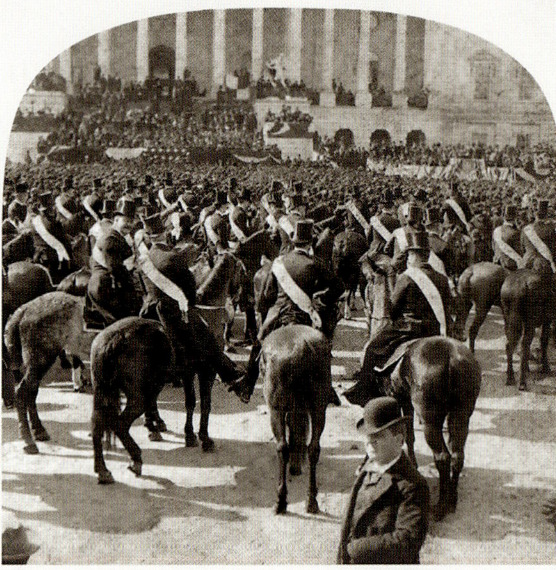

Inauguration of President McKinley

President McKinley and Admiral Dewey

In 1899, Admiral Dewey returned triumphant from the victory of Manila Bay to a ceremony in Washington where he was hailed as the returning hero and presented with a magnificent jeweled sword. By special act of Congress Dewey was made Admiral of the Navy and the Dewey Medal was named in his honor to be presented to members of the U.S. Navy and Marine Corps who had participated in the Battle of Manila Bay. There was a spectacular parade down Pennsylvania Avenue with roofs and windows along the thoroughfare decorated with flags, bunting, and Dewey emblems. The American victories of the Spanish-American War became a source of enormous popularity for McKinley and Dewey.

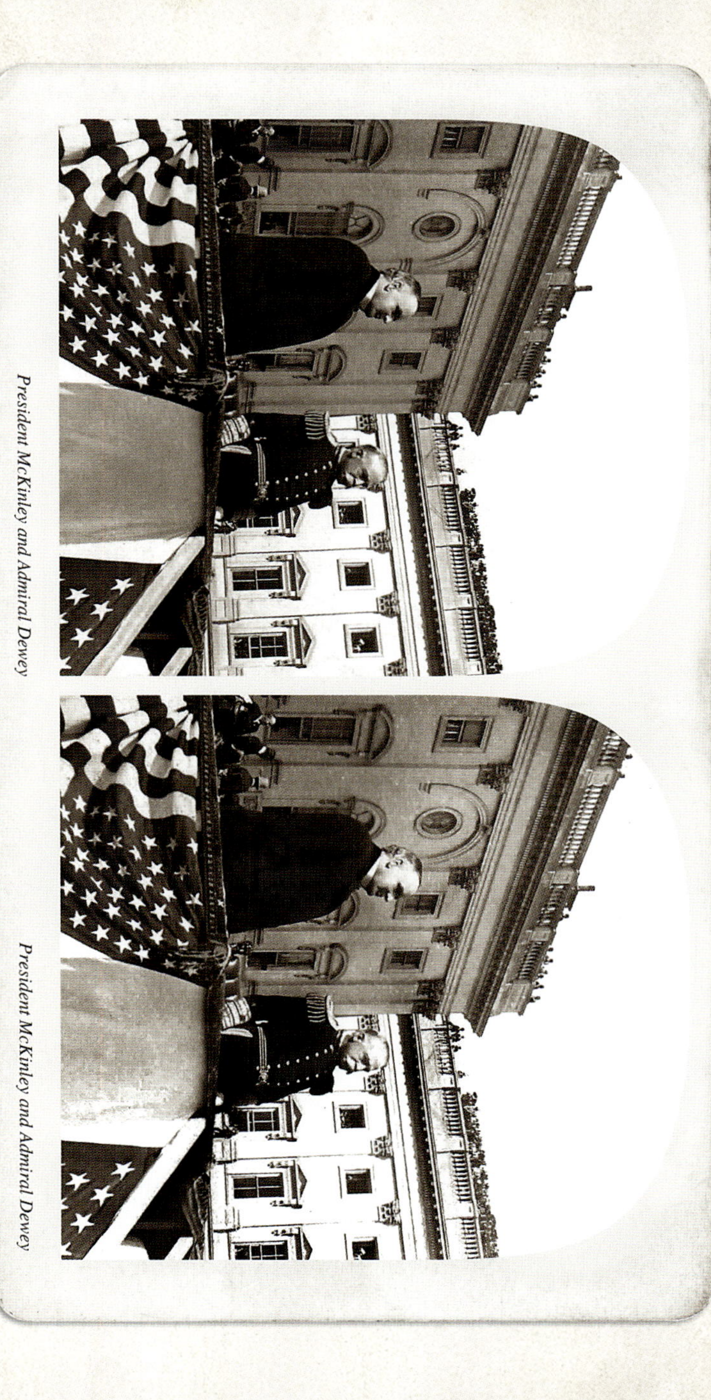
President McKinley and Admiral Dewey
President McKinley and Admiral Dewey

The District of Columbia Vols, returning from Cuba, Marching to the President's Mansion

The Spanish-American War, waged in the spring and summer of 1898, involved Spain's colonial forces in Cuba and the Philippines. Spain's attempt to suppress a revolt in Cuba was one cause of the war, which was further sparked by the explosion of the battleship USS *Maine* in Havana harbor on February 15, 1898. In April of that year, a nationwide call for 125,000 volunteers was issued by President William McKinley. The war ended with the signing of the Treaty of Peace in Paris by U.S. and Spanish representatives on December 10, 1898, with Spain renouncing its rights to Cuba, ceding Puerto Rico and Guam to the United States, and selling the Philippines to the United States.

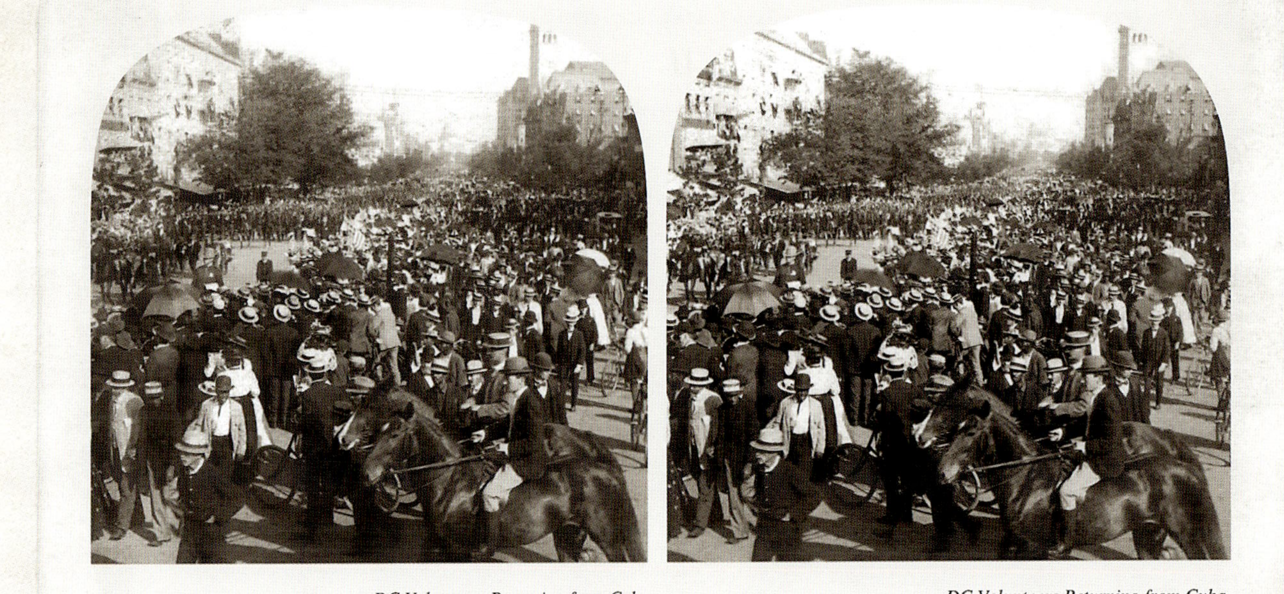

DC Volunteers Returning from Cuba

DC Volunteers Returning from Cuba

East Gun Carriage Shop, Navy Yard

The Washington Navy Yard was established in 1799 and in 1803 it became the home port for the U.S. naval fleet. It is the U.S. Navy's oldest shore establishment. It was used for shipbuilding and also manufactured various other items used on the ships such as chains, cables, and ordnance. This shop was for building gun carriages and gun mounts. In the nineteenth century, the Washington Navy Yard was a major manufacturing establishment. During the War of 1812 the Yard was an important support facility and vital strategic factor in the defense of Washington. To prevent it from being captured by the British, Commodore Tingey ordered the Yard burnt. The Yard never regained its importance as it was thought too far from the open sea, and because the Anacostia River was too shallow for larger modern ships. In more recent times the Navy Yard served as the port for Theodore Roosevelt's presidential yacht, *Mayflower*, and President Roosevelt visited on several occasions to board the yacht.

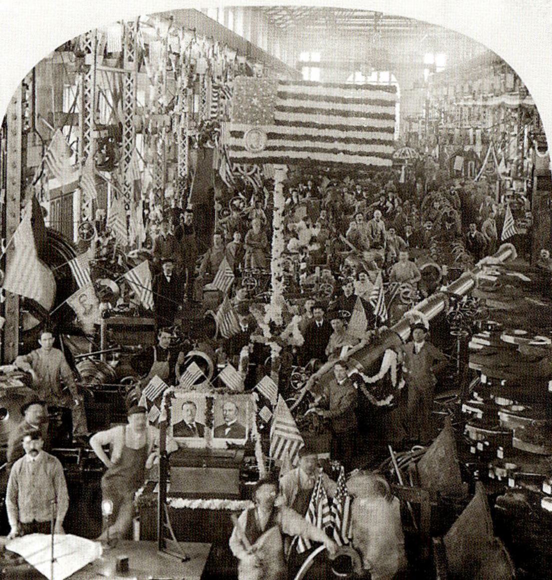

East Gun Carriage Shop, Navy Yard

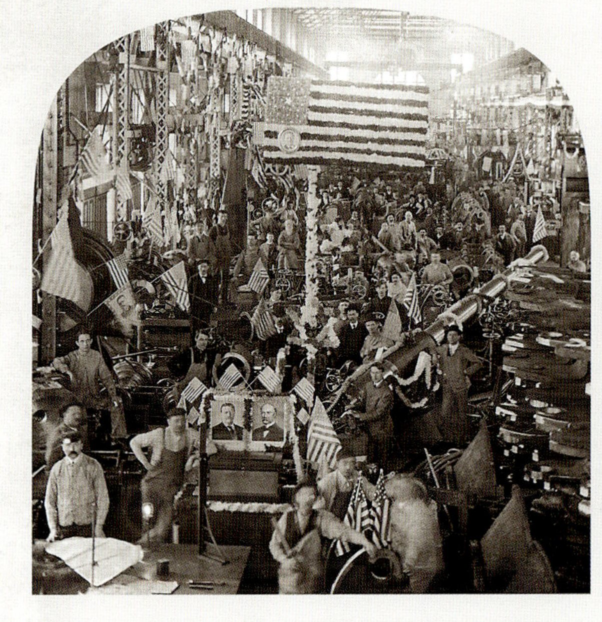

East Gun Carriage Shop, Navy Yard

Tribute to McKinley's Memory

In the western gallery of the House of Representatives, Secretary of State John Hay is giving his famous eulogy for President McKinley on February 27, 1902 (also the twentieth anniversary of James G. Blaine's eulogy for President Garfield). McKinley was shot on September 6, 1901 in Buffalo, New York. This tribute brought together the two houses of Congress with the Cabinet, the Justices of the Supreme Court, the Diplomatic Corps, representatives of the Army and Navy, and distinguished guests, including Prince Henry of Prussia. President Roosevelt sits in the front row of seats directly facing the speaker. Secretary Hay's address was universally pronounced a splendid eulogy of his former chief and friend.

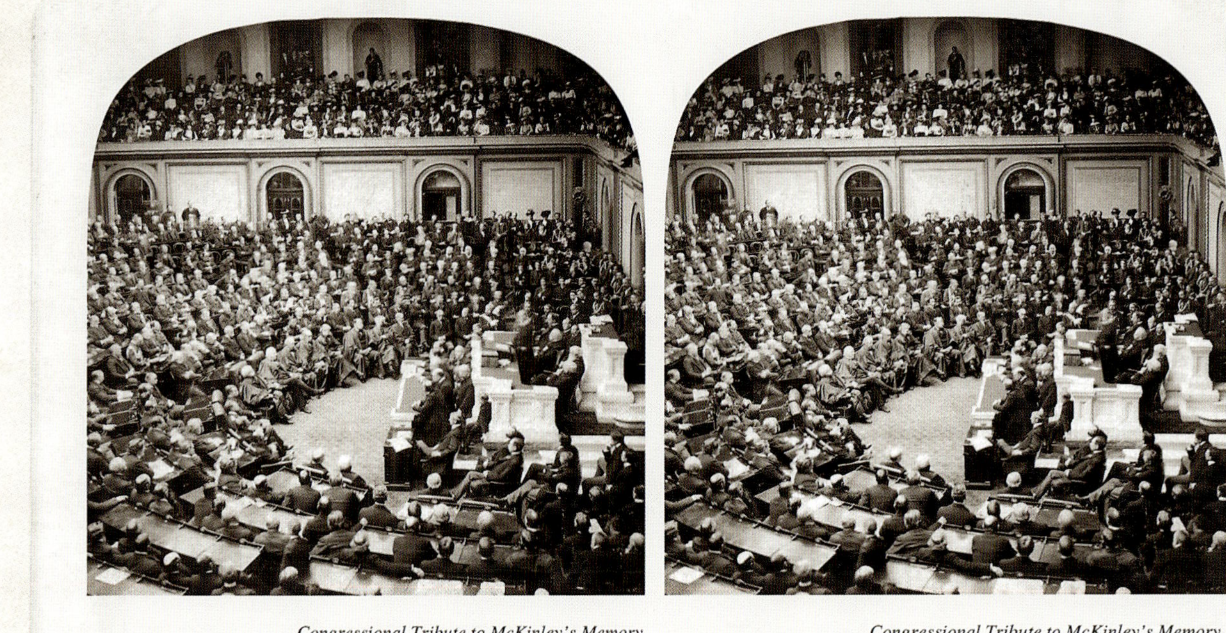

Congressional Tribute to McKinley's Memory

Congressional Tribute to McKinley's Memory

Capitol Dome at Night

The Capitol building, with its majestic proportions, stands as an architectural symbol of America's government. Following new additions to the Capitol in the mid-nineteenth century, the original dome was deemed too small in proportion and in 1856 it was removed and replaced with a fireproof, cast iron dome designed by Philadelphia architect Thomas U. Walter. Upon removing the old dome, a temporary wooden roof was installed over the rotunda with a central hole so that a steam-powered boom and derrick could lift the heavy cast iron into place. When, in 1859, it was discovered that Thomas Crawford's sculpture for the top of the dome, *Statue of Freedom*, was, at 19.5 feet, three feet higher than expected, the dome had to be lowered and flattened. In 1863, the *Statue of Freedom* was lifted atop the dome as gun salutes were fired.